Journeying with Matthew

Available in the Journeying With Series

JOURNEYING WITH MATTHEW

Reflections on the Gospel

James Woodward, Paula Gooder
and Mark Pryce

WESTMINSTER
JOHN KNOX PRESS
LOUISVILLE · KENTUCKY

First published in Great Britain in 2013 as *Journeying with Matthew: Lectionary Year A* by Society for Promoting Christian Knowledge.

Published in the United States of America in 2016 by
Westminster John Knox Press
100 Witherspoon Street
Louisville, KY 40202

16 17 18 19 20 21 22 23 24 25—10 9 8 7 6 5 4 3 2 1

Cover design by Eric Walljasper
Cover art: © Eric Walljasper
Typeset by Graphicraft Limited, Hong Kong

Library of Congress Cataloging-in-Publication Data

Names: Woodward, James, 1961- author.
Title: Journeying with Matthew : reflections on the gospel / James Woodward, Paula Gooder, and Mark Pryce.
Description: Louisville, KY : Westminster John Knox Press, 2016. | Series: Journeying with series | Includes bibliographical references.
Identifiers: LCCN 2015041747 (print) | LCCN 2015042893 (ebook) | ISBN 9780664260217 (alk. paper) | ISBN 9781611646627 (ebook)
Subjects: LCSH: Bible. Matthew--Criticism, interpretation, etc. | Church year. | Common lectionary (1992).
Classification: LCC BS2575.52 .W66 2016 (print) | LCC BS2575.52 (ebook) | DDC 226.2/06--dc23
LC record available at http://lccn.loc.gov/2015041747

Most Westminster John Knox Press books are available at special quantity discounts when purchased in bulk by corporations, organizations, and special-interest groups. For more information, please e-mail SpecialSales@wjkbooks.com.

To Clare and Alan Amos, with appreciation and respect

'Therefore every scribe who has been trained for
the kingdom of heaven is like the master of
a household who brings out of his treasure
what is new and what is old.'
Matthew 13.52

Contents

Preface: What is this book about?

The Revised Common Lectionary has established itself both in Anglican parishes and other denominations as the framework within which the Bible is read on Sundays in public worship. It follows a three-year pattern, taking each of the Synoptic Gospels and reading substantial parts of them in the cycle of the liturgical year. While each of the three years is dedicated in turn to readings from Matthew, Mark and Luke, during parts of the year extensive use is made of John, which will be the subject of the fourth and final volume in this series.

All three authors have extensive experience of reading, preaching, leading, learning and teaching within this framework. We have worked in a variety of contexts: universities, theological colleges, parishes, chaplaincies and religious communities. We share a passion for theological learning that is collaborative, inclusive, intelligent and transformative. This shared concern brought us together across our participation in various aspects of the life of the Diocese of Birmingham in 2007. We started a conversation about how best we might help individuals and groups understand and use the Gospels. We aspired to provide a short resource for Christians in busy and distracted lives so that the Gospel narrative might be explained, illuminated and interpreted for discipleship and service.

This third volume has grown out of our conversations about Matthew. We hope that it will enable readers (alone or in groups) to get a flavour of Matthew's Gospel: to understand something about the events that caused it to be written in the first place; to enter into the shape of the Gospel in the form that the lectionary presents it to us; to enter imaginatively into its life, its concerns and its message; and in so doing to encounter afresh the story of Jesus and, like the disciples on the mountain in Galilee (Matthew 28.17), to worship even in the midst of the doubts that so often crowd around us.

The present book has emerged out of shared study and reflection, during which we attended to the text of the Gospel and examined how best to break open its character, with the intention of offering a mixture of information, interpretation and reflection on life experience in the light of faith. To this end Paula Gooder provides an introduction to the biblical text, Mark Pryce offers creative interpretations of each theme and James Woodward offers a range of styles of reflection. We have all been able to comment on and shape each other's contributions. We hope that the material will be used in whatever way might help the learning life of disciples and communities of faith, and expect some of it to provide a base for study days and preparation for teaching and preaching.

Such a short volume as this can make no claim to comprehensiveness. The choice of seasons and texts has been determined by our attention to the liturgical year and shaped by our attempt to present some of the key characteristics of the Gospel.

First we offer a concise introduction to the main characteristics and themes of Matthew's Gospel. Paula helps us into the shape of the Gospel through a discussion of the person of Matthew, his storytelling technique, his vision as a historian and the main theological themes of the Gospel. In the nine subsequent chapters, which follow the major seasons in the cycle of the Church's liturgical year, Paula offers us material to expound the particular style of the Gospel, Mark's theology is distilled into poetry and prose that offers us imaginative spiritual insights grounded in the Gospel messages, while James offers pastoral and practical theological reflections that bring together faith and experience. At the end of each chapter we ask readers to consider this material in the light of their own understanding and experience, with questions that might form the basis of group conversation and study. A prayer shaped by the theme of the chapter invites further contemplation of the Gospel text as it is rooted in faith and discipleship.

Throughout the book our aim has been to wear our scholarship lightly so that the book is both accessible and stimulating. We make no claim to comprehensiveness: for the sake of clarity and brevity we have been selective in our choice of themes. At the end of the book we offer some resources for further learning.

We hope that you will find this book useful, building on the previous volumes on the Gospels of Mark and Luke, and that it will give you a glimpse of how much we have gained from our collaboration on this project. We thank Ruth McCurry, our editor, for her trust and forbearance. We also thank all those people and communities that have enriched, informed and challenged our responses to the Gospel.

James Woodward
Paula Gooder
Mark Pryce

Introduction: Getting to know the Gospel of Matthew

Exploring the text

Matthew's Gospel sometimes evokes a mixed response from its readers, much more so than either Mark or Luke. While Matthew's Gospel contains iconic and well-loved episodes such as the visit of the Magi (2.1) or the Sermon on the Mount (chapters 5—7), it also includes some much more difficult passages. For example, in Matthew people are more often condemned either to the outer darkness or to the furnace of fire where there will be weeping and gnashing of teeth. Matthew's Gospel contains the apparently brutal parable of the wedding banquet, in which a guest is evicted from the feast simply for wearing the wrong clothes (22.12–13), as well as, in chapter 23, a long string of woes against the Pharisees. As a result of passages like these, Matthew's Gospel can feel condemnatory as well as encouraging; harsh as well as loving. All in all it is a more challenging Gospel.

This raises the question of why it has a harsher edge. Why is it that the Gospel seems to be so much more critical of those around? Why is judgement so near to the surface? Why does it appear so harsh so often? Scholars have often answered this question by exploring the audience and context of the Gospel, so this seems a good place from which to begin our exploration of Matthew.

Who was Matthew?

The first question to ask as we explore the issue of the audience and context of a Gospel is, of course, who wrote it? Traditionally, the first canonical Gospel was attributed to someone called Matthew. This association was made fairly early on in the life of the Gospel by Papias, a bishop in Hierapolis (in modern Turkey), possibly as early as 125 AD.

The same view was repeated by Irenaeus (*c.* 130–200), Bishop of Lyons, around 50 years later. By the end of the second century, that Matthew was clearly linked in people's minds with the Matthew who was named as one of the Twelve in Matthew's Gospel and identified as a former tax collector (Matthew 9.9; 10.3).

This identification immediately throws up a problem. In Matthew's Gospel the tax collector is called 'Matthew', whereas in Mark 2.14 and Luke 5.27, in apparently the same story, he is called 'Levi'. There is no agreement among scholars about why this might be the case. Options include the two stories being similar but not the same (so referring to two different people); the man having two names, one known by Matthew's readers and the other by Mark and Luke; there being no reference to a Levi who was one of Jesus' disciples but there is one to a Matthew and so the two characters were conflated; or that the author of Matthew's Gospel was this person and he preferred to refer to himself by a different name. In reality, there is no good explanation for the change, and the reason why he is called Matthew in one Gospel and Levi in two others remains a mystery.

Tax collectors

It is much clearer, however, that this person, Matthew or Levi, was known as a tax or toll collector. It is clear from elsewhere in the Gospels that tax collectors were hated. Many people ascribe this hatred to a corrupt taxation system known as tax farming. For many years the Roman Empire used the system, adopted from the Greek city states, which allowed tax collectors (known in Latin as *Publicani* and hence called publicans in the KJV) to buy from the empire the right to collect taxes. This meant that they paid the Romans a fixed fee which gave them permission to collect tax. They often recouped this fee many times over by charging extortionate rates of tax in the region where they were collectors.

Julius Caesar, however, had outlawed tax farming, so that by Jesus' time the system was no longer used. Instead the Romans paid officials to collect the tax directly. As a result the hatred felt for tax collectors might have been historic, or might simply have arisen because they worked directly for the Romans or because they collected what was perceived to be an unfair tax (it might of course have been all three!).

Of particular interest in the account of the calling of Matthew is the fact that he was sitting at a toll booth in Capernaum when Jesus called him to follow. Capernaum was a crucially important town in Galilee (which probably explains why Jesus chose to relocate there from Nazareth). As well as being a Roman garrison town, Capernaum lay close to the border between Herod Antipas' territory and that of his half-brother Philip the Tetrarch (sometimes also known as Herod Philip). It was also on the trade route between the Roman port of Caesarea and the city of Damascus. As a result, the tax collector in Capernaum would have collected the tolls of those crossing the border between Herod Antipas' territory and Philip's on their way to trade in Damascus. Such a role would have been highly lucrative, which may give us some insight into the nature of a character who could occupy such a profitable, if dangerous, position.

The question remains, however, of how reliable is the tradition that links the author of the first Gospel with Matthew the tax collector. As always, this is a subject upon which scholars take different views and about which each reader must make up his or her own mind. But, for the sake of simplicity, in what follows we will call the author of the Gospel Matthew, following two millennia of Christian tradition.

Matthew as a Jewish Gospel

If there is disagreement about whether the first Gospel was written by a tax collector, there is a much greater level of agreement about the Jewish nature of Matthew's Gospel. The same Papias who declared that the author of the Gospel was called Matthew, also declared that its author collected the sayings of Jesus (or about Jesus) in the Hebrew language (or in the Hebrew style).

On one level this raises problems. Even the earliest manuscripts of the Gospel are in Greek, but more importantly the Gospel gives no indication that it was translated. It contains more Hebraisms (i.e. stylistic quirks that someone who spoke Hebrew or Aramaic may have introduced into the Greek text*) than the other Gospels, but not so many as to suggest that it was first written in Hebrew or Aramaic and then translated. The Hebraisms include turns of phrase like saying that the Magi 'rejoiced with great joy', which has been smoothed out in the NRSV to 'they were overwhelmed with joy' (Matthew 2.10). Such turns of phrase are characteristically Semitic and suggest the author might have been thinking in Hebrew or Aramaic, even if not writing in it.

So we are left with the question of what Papias meant when he said that Matthew collected the sayings of Jesus in the Hebrew language. Did he, perhaps, collect the sayings of Jesus that had been preserved in the Hebrew language? Or perhaps he wrote an earlier collection in Hebrew/Aramaic which was then rewritten into the Gospel. It is almost impossible to tell. One option is that Papias' phrase should be translated not as 'Hebrew language' but 'Hebrew style'; thus he would be saying that Matthew wrote from a Jewish perspective and with a Jewish audience in mind. This much seems clear. Matthew's Gospel is evidently Hebrew in tone. Its theology has Hebraic resonances; it rarely explains any Jewish practices and it draws heavily on the Old Testament.

---

* Aramaic is the language that became the 'lingua franca' or everyday language in the Babylonian and subsequent empires. It is a Semitic language, and therefore is very similar to Hebrew, but was spoken outside Israel for many years. At the time of Jesus, although Greek was now the language of the empire, people in Israel spoke Aramaic every day and used Hebrew only for worship.

Indeed Matthew's use of the Old Testament is fascinating. Matthew refers to the Old Testament in a variety of ways:

- Sometimes he quotes directly from the Greek translation of the Old Testament (also known as the Septuagint or LXX). For example, Matthew 21.16 cites Psalm 8.2 as 'Out of the mouths of infants and nursing babies you have prepared praise for yourself'. Here the LXX reads the same, 'have prepared praise', but the Hebrew reads instead 'you have established might'. So in this instance it is clear he is quoting from the LXX.

- Sometimes he retranslates the Old Testament into Greek from Hebrew. For example, Matthew 11.29 reads 'Take my yoke upon you, and learn from me; for I am gentle and humble in heart, and you will find rest for your souls.' This is a quotation from Jeremiah 6.16; in the LXX it reads 'and you will find purification for your souls', whereas the Hebrew like Matthew reads 'and you will find rest for your souls'. So here it is clear that Matthew was using the Hebrew text.

- Sometimes he uses composite quotations taken from different places in the Old Testament. For example Matthew 27.9–10 quotes what is said to be Jeremiah in the context of Judas' receiving 30 pieces of silver. The passage reads: 'Then was fulfilled what had been spoken through the prophet Jeremiah, "And they took the thirty pieces of silver, the price of the one on whom a price had been set, on whom some of the people of Israel had set a price, and they gave them for the potter's field, as the Lord commanded me",' which combines Jeremiah 18.12 and 32.8–9 with Zechariah 11.12–13.

- Occasionally he even attributes a quote to the Old Testament that is not easy to find. For example, Matthew 2.23 states that he made 'his home in a town called Nazareth, so that what had been spoken through the prophets might be fulfilled, "He will be called a Nazorean."' The quotation is best explained as a Semitic play on words using the Hebrew word for branch, which if transliterated from Hebrew into Aramaic and then into Greek could end up in a form similar to Nazorean. This throws up the possibility that Matthew was not referring to the Old Testament but quoting from memory, and that he knew both the Greek and the Hebrew versions of the Old Testament but sometimes muddled them (and indeed the names of the prophets) up.

It has been said that an argument against Matthew being Jewish comes towards the end of the Gospel with the triumphal entry into Jerusalem. Here we encounter a somewhat odd detail: Jesus sends his disciples to find 'a donkey tied, and a colt with her'. This, Matthew makes clear, is in fulfilment of Zechariah 9.9:

> Rejoice greatly, O daughter Zion!
> Shout aloud, O daughter Jerusalem!
> Lo, your king comes to you; triumphant and victorious
>   is he,
> humble and riding on a donkey, on a colt, the foal of
>   a donkey.

As a result Matthew 21.7 has Jesus riding on both the donkey and the colt simultaneously (a feat that has challenged many people's imaginations). Someone from the Hebrew tradition would probably have known that Zechariah was employing Hebrew parallelism here, in which the same point is made twice, whereas Matthew appears to assume that two different animals are involved – a donkey and a colt. Odd as this detail is, it does not detract from the rest of the Hebraic nature of the rest of the Gospel and may be put down to Matthew's tendency to provide extravagant images for effect (e.g. at Jesus' crucifixion in Matthew 27.51–52, not only is the veil of the Temple torn in two as in the other two Gospels, but there is also an earthquake that allows the dead to rise).

One of the most strikingly Hebraic features of Matthew's Gospel is the portrayal of Jesus as a new Moses, and possibly the Gospel itself as a new Torah. It is important not to press these resonances too far, but we can observe some fascinating similarities. The Gospel begins with a genealogy – similar to many of those in the Torah – and indeed the opening sentence declares that this is a '*biblos geneseōs*' of Jesus Christ, using the same word as the Greek name, 'Genesis', of the first book of the Bible.

Also interesting are the parallels between Jesus' birth and that of Moses: born into a hostile environment, his parents are forced to take extreme action to save the life of the newborn baby and must leave Egypt to enable the salvation of God's people. The way in which Matthew recounts the birth narratives brings to mind on more than one occasion the infancy of Moses. Much more important still, however, is the Sermon on the Mount. Here, as in Exodus, the law is given on a mountain. As in Exodus the commandments that will shape the lived reality of God's people are given by a man, and in Matthew this man is Jesus – the new Moses.

In the light of all of this it is interesting that the Gospel is clearly five-fold in structure (like the five-fold structure of the Torah), with the addition of a prologue that contains the beginning of Jesus' life and an epilogue that contains his end and subsequent resurrection. Each of the five principal units seems to have two elements: a major narrative, followed by a discourse. Furthermore, each unit begins in a similar way, which translated into English reads 'When Jesus had . . .' (see Matthew 8.1; 11.1; 13.53; 19.1).

The structure of the Gospel appears to be like this:

- prologue: genealogy, nativity and infancy narratives [Matthew 1—2];
- first narrative (the baptism of Jesus) and discourse (the Sermon on the Mount) [Matthew 3—7];

- second narrative (three miracles with two stories of discipleship) and discourse (focusing on mission and suffering) [Matthew 8—10];
- third narrative (conflict with Jesus' opponents) and discourse (a series of parables) [Matthew 11—13.52];
- fourth narrative (increasing opposition to Jesus) and discourse (preparation of the disciples for Jesus' absence) [Matthew 13.53—18];
- fifth narrative (Jesus travels to Jerusalem) and discourse (the coming end) [Matthew 19.1—20];
- epilogue: the last week of Jesus' life, death, resurrection and great commission [Matthew 21—28].

Like all attempts to discern the structure of biblical books, this list comes with the caveat that some of the units are more obvious than others. For example, the first narrative and discourse, which contains Jesus' baptism followed by the Sermon on the Mount, seems very clear indeed; whereas subsequent ones, such as the third narrative and discourse, are less easy to perceive. Nevertheless, there is a growing consensus among scholars that Matthew's Gospel can be seen to have five key parts. Given the Hebraic tone of the rest of the Gospel – and particularly its emphasis on Jesus as being a new Moses – it does not seem over-fanciful to draw a connection between the five units of Matthew's Gospel and the five books of the Torah.

Matthew as an anti-Jewish Gospel

It is clear that Matthew's Gospel was written by someone who was Jewish. The author seems to know his Old Testament well, to be portraying Jesus as a new Moses and Jesus' teachings as a new Torah, and to expect his readers to understand Jewish practice. What is unsettling, however, is that Matthew may be both the most Jewish and the most anti-Jewish Gospel. No one can read Matthew 23 and its list of 'woes' – 'Woe to you, scribes and Pharisees, hypocrites!' (23.13, 15, 16, 23, 25, 27, 29) –

without feelings of profound unease. Jesus' criticism of the scribes and Pharisees in this chapter is more vehement than in any other Gospel. He condemns them for a wide range of evils, from hypocrisy to leading people astray, from loving the Temple's money more than the Temple itself to paying attention to minutiae and missing the point of the law. On and on the chapter goes, flaying the scribes and Pharisees for a wide range of sins.

This raises the question of why this condemnation is so much more bitter in Matthew than elsewhere. The explanation often given by scholars is that such hostility tells us a lot about the community to which Matthew was writing.

Scholars who express an interest in Matthew's community often use a technique known as 'redaction criticism' to read the Gospel. The term redaction is taken from the German term *Redaktion*, which means simply 'editing'. The premise from which such theories begin is that when Matthew wrote his Gospel he used one or more sources: Mark, possibly the hypothetical source 'Q', and his own material, which scholars often call 'M'. Redaction criticism pays attention to the small details where Matthew's Gospel is noticeably different from those of Mark and Luke and puts them together to see if the picture that emerges can tell us something about the changes that Matthew made to his sources.

The parting of the ways between Judaism and Christianity

One interesting feature to emerge from this process is that, alongside the negative comments about the scribes and Pharisees that we have already identified, there are a number of references which refer to 'their synagogues':

- Matthew 4.23: 'Jesus went throughout Galilee, teaching in their synagogues and proclaiming the good news of the kingdom and curing every disease and every sickness among the people.'

- Matthew 9.35: 'Then Jesus went about all the cities and villages, teaching in their synagogues, and proclaiming the good news of the kingdom.'
- Matthew 10.17: 'Beware of them, for they will hand you over to councils and flog you in their synagogues.'

This might appear to be a small detail, but in a Gospel that is so clearly Jewish in origin and probably written for a Jewish audience it becomes a very important one. Why would Matthew refer to 'their synagogues'? The best explanation that scholars have found is that he is differentiating between 'their synagogues' and 'our synagogues'.

For much of the twentieth century, scholars assumed that there was a final and dramatic split between the Rabbinic Jewish community and the Jewish Christian community after the fall of the Temple in AD 70. After the Romans were victorious in the Jewish war, they destroyed the Temple in Jerusalem. This was an astute move if they wanted to subjugate the Jewish people. The Temple had been the symbolic unifying factor within Judaism. As a result, many diverse groups (the Pharisees, the Sadducees, the Essenes, etc.) were able to coexist within Judaism thanks to the unifying pull exerted by the Temple.

Once the Temple was destroyed, this unifying force no longer existed and Judaism had to find a new form of self-definition. For much of the twentieth century, scholars believed that the Jewish leaders thereafter convened a council in Jamnia (known in Hebrew as Yavneh) out of which they made various promulgations. One of these was a set of 18 prayers or benedictions to be recited by faithful Jews throughout the day. The twelfth prayer was thought to include a cursing of Christians, and this, scholars believed, marked a 'parting of the ways' between Judaism and Christianity.

More recent scholarship recognizes that this is an exaggeration of the evidence. There is no evidence of a council at Jamnia at which promulgations were made. The 18 benedictions, otherwise known as the *Amidah*, remain at the heart of Jewish liturgy but it is clear that they are not focused on Christians. Only one of the 18 prayers has anything to do with Christians and the word used there is 'minim', which means sectarians or heretics. While it clearly includes Christians, there is nothing to suggest that it was directed solely against them.

Nevertheless, the period following the fall of the Temple was one in which Judaism sought to redefine itself. One of the markers of this redefinition was a much greater clarity about what counted as Judaism and what did not. There is now strong evidence that Jewish Christians retained their Jewish identity and often continued attending their local synagogue well into the fourth century AD, if not beyond. But at the same time there was conflict during this period between the Rabbis, who sought to redefine Judaism, particularly in terms of a renewed focus on the Torah, and the Jewish Christians, who sought to redefine Judaism in terms of a focus on Jesus Christ.

Scholars discern in Matthew's Gospel not anti-Semitism (which can only happen in groups that are not Jewish) but a struggle between two Jewish groups as to what did and did not count as Judaism. If you recognize that Matthew's Gospel is profoundly Jewish, then what he is doing is redefining Judaism around Jesus Christ. His portrayal of Jesus as the new Moses, giving a new law on a new mountain, points his followers to a radical new way of being Jewish which centres not on the Temple or on Torah but on Jesus Christ. His profound criticism of the scribes and Pharisees, who claim to lead the people correctly but whom he believes to be hypocritical and shallow, can be seen as a sideswipe at the leaders of a rival group within Judaism.

Where and when was the Gospel written?

Exploring what Matthew's community might have looked like inevitably brings us to the question of where the Gospel might have been written. This too is very difficult to answer. Christian tradition points to Antioch, in Syria, but the source of the Gospel could have been any major town or city in which there were large enough groups of Jews to spark a conflict between Matthew's community and those who believed that Judaism must be expressed in a different way. Given that Judaism's period of self-definition was focused in the late first century following the fall of the Temple, many scholars believe that this is the most likely date for its composition (probably in the mid to late 70s AD); others, though, would argue that the period of conflict was earlier, not after the fall of the Temple but before it, around the time when the Jewish war began (AD 66–72). If this is correct then Matthew's Gospel may date from around the late 60s AD.

Matthew's Gospel may be an uncomfortable read at times but if you scratch below the surface and exercise historical imagination, it becomes possible to imagine a context in which this kind of language and expression become understandable. If Matthew's community was experiencing severe pressure from other Jewish groups, then it would be unsurprising for Matthew to strike back with a clearly articulated view of why his form of Judaism was not only defensible but a proper way of worshipping the God of heaven and earth.

If scholars are correct in their view of Matthew's community, then Matthew's Gospel, perhaps more than any of the others, offers us a snapshot not just of Jesus' life but also of the life of an early Christian community as they tried to work out who they were and what following Jesus meant.

1

Advent

———•◦•———

Exploring the text

Matthew is a good Gospel for Advent. It contrasts strongly with Mark, which is profoundly unhelpful in Advent. Barely has Mark's Gospel begun before John the Baptist and Jesus burst onto the scene and begin the story in earnest. Matthew's Gospel is very different and builds up the picture much more slowly and patiently, reminding its readers not only of the importance of waiting but of how long God's people had waited for this moment.

The genealogy

It is hardly surprising that the compilers of the Lectionary opted not to include Matthew's genealogy in the readings – even the most talented reader would struggle to make it interesting when read out in church. Nevertheless, the genealogy of Matthew is very important during Advent since it focuses our attention on waiting. The point that Matthew wishes to emphasize in these opening verses is how far back Jesus' roots went. In the face of his detractors, who claimed that he was changing Judaism, bringing new ideas and, maybe, failing to understand what Judaism really was, Matthew took care to show that Jesus' origins stretched as far back as the father of Judaism himself.

The purpose of biblical genealogies is always theological rather than historical. In an age without electoral rolls, census data and historical records offices, it was impossible either to prove or disprove genealogical claims of this kind. Even to raise the question of their historicity is to miss the point. This is emphasized by the fact that the genealogy is traced via Joseph who, Matthew makes clear, is not Jesus' biological father.* Apparently this caused no problems at all in Matthew's mind, even though it raises many questions for us today, and probably gives us a clue about the symbolic power of legal paternity in the ancient world. Once accepted in Joseph's family, Jesus' line *was* that of Joseph, whether his genes were biologically of that line or not. In the genealogy Matthew is making some vitally important theological points, all intended to demonstrate that Jesus was embedded deep within the story of God's salvation.

A couple of noteworthy features of the genealogy re-emphasize this point. The first is that Matthew locates Jesus in the story of the key moments of God's salvation in history. The genealogy enables Matthew to mention not only Abraham but David, Hezekiah and Josiah, all kings who sought to bring God's people back to themselves and to proper worship of God.

A second feature of the genealogy is that it is themed in three lots of 14 generations (a double perfect number), demonstrating that Jesus' birth occurred at an opportune time. Both the story into which he was born and the time at which his birth took place pointed to Jesus being the 'One' so long awaited. If we look at the three lots of 14 this becomes even clearer. The first 14 end with David; the second with the exile; the third with the birth of the Messiah. Matthew is pointing out that God had intervened to save his people after 14 generations, first with David and then through the exile. Now the time was ripe for him to do so again.

We cannot leave the genealogy without pausing for a moment to notice its oddest feature. Woven within it are five women:

---

* A similar dynamic also functions in Luke, who also presents a genealogy via Joseph but does so through an entirely different line (not Solomon but Nathan) and even gives Joseph a different father (Heli not Jacob). Again this emphasizes that the theological point is far more important here than the biological one.

Tamar, Rahab, Ruth, Bathsheba and Mary. It is extremely unusual to find women included in genealogies where the family tree is traced exclusively down the male line. Inevitably there has been substantial discussion among scholars as to why the five should be included here. There is no agreed answer but the most favoured solution is that all five are slightly dubious (some more so than others). Tamar disguised herself as a 'harlot' and conceived her twins by her father-in-law; Rahab was a 'harlot' and saved God's people in Jericho; Ruth, a foreigner from the much hated Moab, seduced Boaz on the threshing floor; Bathsheba, mother of Solomon, committed adultery with King David; and Mary conceived Jesus outside wedlock (albeit by the action of the Holy Spirit). The presence of Mary's four predecessors suggests that Matthew is subtly defending Jesus' reputation against criticism that his irregular conception rules him out of being able to save God's people. Matthew demonstrates that God's story of salvation has always contained irregularities, women whose actions might be considered by some to be reprehensible but which, in fact, allowed God's salvation to come about. Jesus' birth might be irregular but this does not detract from the salvation he has brought.

John the Baptist

John the Baptist symbolizes in Matthew this long period of waiting for the one who would come to save God's people. He has a much bigger role in Matthew than in any of the other Gospels, where he is mentioned largely in passing. In Matthew, however, we begin to glimpse the significance of this prophetic, troubling character. On one level, John's portrayal is very similar to that we find in the other Gospels. He is an Elijah-type figure, living in the wilderness, dressed, as Elijah was in 2 Kings 1.8, in camel hair with a belt around his waist. He is clearly the precursor of Christ and is linked, as he is in all the Gospels, with 'the voice crying in the wilderness' (Isaiah 40).

The significance of the use of this passage from Isaiah is that the voice in the wilderness was preparing for God's return to his people. In the exile, God had abandoned the Temple, and his people with it, because of their actions and their betrayal of the covenant relationship. In Isaiah 40, the prophet recognizes that God will return but that the people must be prepared for it. John the Baptist's location in the wilderness by the Jordan not only symbolized God's return across the desert to his people but also the very first entry into the land with Joshua. Going out to the wilderness represented not just the leaving of everyday life but a very specific summoning outwards to the spot where it all first began and would begin again. Jesus' own baptism there was the symbol that this great event, the moment when God's people could truly return from exile in the company of their saviour, had begun.

John the Baptist is often presented as the precursor of Jesus – as he is in Mark and Luke – but in Matthew he becomes more than this. One of the striking features of Matthew's account of John the Baptist is that John proclaims, 'Repent, for the kingdom of heaven has come near' (Matthew 3.2), exactly the same thing that Jesus proclaims in Matthew 4.17. John is not simply the precursor of Jesus like the other prophets but is the inaugurator of a new age, proclaiming what Jesus is also to proclaim. Nevertheless, John has an ambiguous relationship with this new age. He inaugurated the new age but, as Jesus makes clear in Matthew 11.11 ('the least in the kingdom of heaven is greater than he'), he was not part of it. He stood on the threshold, proclaimed the message of Jesus, but never became a part of this new kingdom.

Many scholars believe that this was the case not because John was unimportant, but because he was so very important. Josephus, the Jewish historian, reports with approval in *Antiquities* 18.116–19 that John the Baptist 'was a good man and had exhorted the Jews to lead righteous lives'. This, along with the evidence in Acts (and John's Gospel) that the followers of John the Baptist remained together long after his death, suggests that it was vital to Matthew to present John as important (because he was) but very much not a part of the new era of Christ. John then becomes someone who stands on the threshold between the old and the new; prophetic in style but proclaiming the message of the kingdom just as Jesus did.

The end of the age

As we are beginning to see, Matthew's Gospel presents Jesus as the beginning of a new age. The genealogy in chapter 1 presents the history of God's people in three lots of 14 generations, the implication being that now was the opportune moment for a new era to begin. John the Baptist stands perfectly balanced on the cusp of this new era, symbolizing the prophets of old but speaking the words of Jesus and inaugurating the new era. In Advent we reflect on this new age, inaugurated by John and lived out in Jesus, but we also look forward to yet another new age: the new age that Jesus and his disciples talked about in Matthew 24.

The theme of the coming of the new age often leads to a sense of discomfort during Advent. This is partially because those who love this theme too much spend hours speculating on whether or not the precise signs of the end portrayed in Matthew can be found in contemporary events. This is hardly a new phenomenon: in times of great stress throughout the whole of Christian history, people have speculated about whether or not contemporary events are a sign of the end. To do so, however, is to misunderstand what Jesus says in Matthew 24. The point of the passage is not the signs of the end but the waiting for the Son of Man to return. The signs of the end are given so that you will know that it is worth enduring through them as you wait for the much greater moment when the Son of Man will come. Matthew 24 is, like many similar passages, a bizarre message of hope. Laying out the disasters that will

come is designed to encourage us all to endure, to look beyond
them and to keep our eyes fixed in hope on the one who will
come – to borrow words from the book of Revelation, to wipe
all tears from our eyes.

Matthew's Gospel reminds us all that we are to become
figures like John the Baptist, drawing people out from where
they are to a place in which they, and we, can truly prepare for
the coming of God's kingdom on earth.

Imagining the text

A distinctive feature of the birth narrative in Matthew 1 and 2 is
the way in which Joseph is foregrounded in the story of Jesus'
nativity and early childhood. Joseph is not a bystander, separated
from the action, but through his relationship with Jesus and his
mother Mary is given a key role in welcoming and safeguarding
God's purposes of salvation for the whole world. The Advent poem
below, and the two that follow in Christmas and Epiphany – the
seasons celebrating the incarnation and revelation of God in
Jesus Christ – reflect on the role of Joseph as it is told in Matthew's
Gospel, and on what insights the character and actions of Joseph
offer into the nature of God's calling and the kinds of human
response which his discipleship shows.

Another distinctive feature of Matthew is the genealogy which
opens the Gospel. Unlike conventional Jewish genealogies,
this family tree contains women as well as men, and four of the
women named are extraordinary; they are foreigners (non-Jews)
and in one sense, sinners. Tamar, who seduced her father-in-
law Judah (Genesis 38); Rahab, a prostitute (Joshua 2.1–21;
6.17–25); Bathsheba, who committed adultery with King David
(2 Samuel 11); and Ruth the Moabite, who enticed Boaz (Ruth 3).
The inclusion of these women in the genealogy of God's Messiah
celebrates the purpose of God to bless all the nations of the
earth through a Messiah descended from Abraham, and suggests

that Mary's son, conceived and born outside wedlock, is another, final expression of God's grace. In this history of salvation Joseph is named as the 'husband of Mary', emphasizing that he is not the father of Jesus the Saviour. But this is no disgrace; it is the culmination of God's promise to Abraham, that in Jesus all the world will be blessed.

In this poem Joseph the carpenter thinks about the ways in which different kinds of wood are used in his craft – exotic cedar wood from Lebanon in the Temple, and in his own joinery any timber on which he can lay his hands; both are beautiful and practical. For him this is an analogy for the way God practises the skilled work of salvation – using not only the best material, but also whatever will do the job.

The beauty of country furniture
Though I leave my tools at home,
in the Temple I remain a carpenter.
Prayer is measuring its built dimensions with ecstatic eyes –
the height, length, breadth of hallowed space –
my fingers tracing sacred joinery, the screens
of finest skill.

Most of all it is the wood that heavens me,
solid, aromatic, dark,
cedar shipped from Lebanon,
exquisite, dear, bought with royal Persian gold
to make the carved and chiselled place
where God draws near.

Back in the provinces, making stools and family dressers,
it is the same skills with local timber,
cut from what's to hand in field and coppice –
the oak and pine – which make a home holy
for the sacred outsider: Tamar, Rahab, Bathsheba, Ruth,
even my good wife, Mary.

19

Reflecting on the text

Who are you?

During Advent we are invited to consider John the Baptist and his relationship to Jesus. John the Baptist appears in the tradition of the great prophets, preaching repentance and reform to the people of Israel. John the Baptist is presented as the figure who bridges the time before Christ and prepares the way for Christ's own ministry. John, the bridge person, asks us what we are looking for in this bridge time. John baptizes for repentance and for forgiveness of sins, preparing the way for God's salvation.

I have always been intrigued by family genealogies, encouraged, at least in part, by the BBC series *Who Do You Think You Are?* The programme takes famous people into hidden parts of their family history, often revealing unexplored dimensions of their past. New discoveries, shameful secrets, connections and unanswered questions all play their part in the deeper revelation of a person that viewers thought they knew. Perhaps we are forced to ask the searching question: 'Who are you?'

I wonder what you feel like when you see a photograph of yourself. I know a number of people who claim they always look bad in photographs. Think about seeing a picture of yourself. Perhaps, you think, the person in the photo doesn't look as beautiful, charming, witty or relaxed as I like to believe I look. Either the equipment is faulty or the photographer is hopeless. Or I have a gene that makes me drop all my fine qualities the moment someone points a camera lens at me. Or – try this one – I have the kind of warm and effusive personality that is impossible to capture in a single two-dimensional image. 'Who are you?'

We could simply say, That's what the photograph shows, so I suppose that's what I look like and maybe I should face up to that. But no – instead we say I always look terrible in photographs. I know who I am; no one else does, least of all that cruel, distorting cold-hearted camera.

Perhaps most of us do know who we are. Part of the challenge of Advent might be to ask ourselves upon what that knowledge is based. Of course each of us is unique and precious. In our relationship with God we are held to be more wonderful, more exquisite in looks, character, taste and style than anyone could describe or capture. How then do we communicate that individuality? One feature of our culture with its emphasis on youth, image and strength is our inability to embrace a richer, textured and perhaps more complex picture of who we are. Can we face our darkness, our insecurities, our desires and needs?

A feature of our social network culture, of blogging and Tweeting and Facebooking and its transitory nature, is that it gives us innumerable opportunities to present ourselves to one another at our best. We can live the inside on the outside and remind people what wonderfully exciting lives we lead. And even those of you most committed to Facebook will know what extraordinary things people post on that network for the world to see. I am reminded of a moment in the comedy series *Absolutely Fabulous* when Saffy says to Edina, her mother, 'Stop trying to find yourself fascinating.'

When we are immersed in such a culture of digitally enhanced appearances and fleeting connection, we live on the surface. Our food is fast, our attention span short, and this can lead to a deep-rooted anti-intellectualism in all areas of our living. In such a situation it is very hard to answer the question, 'Who are you?' Instead we are constantly answering the question, 'Who can I persuade people I am?' The people we call successful are often those who have convinced a large number of the public that they are brilliant. Perhaps successful people often find this question, 'Who am I?', particularly hard to answer: they have peddled their publicity so many times that they have started to believe it themselves. Sometimes all a leader has to do is to convince others that he or she looks and sounds good! Success is a drug that makes you think your identity is a product you can market to unwary customers; at the end, of course, the only one we fool is ourselves.

'Who are you?' I wonder what it is in life that helps to give us a deeper understanding of who we truly are.

In Advent we find ourselves abruptly face to face with a man giving testimony, a man called John who sets his stall some way from the centre of Israel, some way from Jerusalem, from the Temple, from the people who decide what is godly – indeed, on the other side of the Jordan, outside the traditional boundaries of the promised land. John doesn't have a website, he doesn't have a Facebook page, and it's hard to know who he is and what he stands for.

The high and mighty send their lackeys to ask John, 'Who are you?' It becomes clear that John is in line with the way God has worked over the centuries and prepared Israel for this moment. Whenever he is asked the question, 'Who are you?' we see that his answer is 'I am not . . .' It is a funny kind of answer and he repeats it several times. There is something aggressive about it. John can only answer the question in relation to Jesus. Think about those words for a moment. When asked 'Who are you?' John responds to his interrogators, 'I cannot answer that question except in relation to Jesus.' What would your answer be?

Here is the core message of this reflection. Without God we do not know who we are. We can discover our ancestors, our home, our tastes, our dreams, our friendships, our sexuality, our favourite colours, our rhythms, our learning styles, our psychological metrics, our DNA, our genes, our voice, our family tree. These can all be helpful in their own way. But none of them really answers the question 'Who are you?' None of them discloses the most important thing about us. Like John, what really matters about us is to what and to whom we are a witness.

And what is a witness? One twentieth-century French spiritual writer, Emmanuel Suhard, had the answer to that question. He wrote: 'To be a witness consists not in engaging in propaganda, nor even in stirring people up, but in being a living mystery. It means to live in such a way that one's life would not make sense if God did not exist.'

That is the answer. John was a mystery to his interrogators. But he knew who he was. He was a living mystery whose life made no sense if Jesus was not about to come among us. Jesus is calling us to be witnesses. Jesus is whispering our memory and imagination into a life that he has searched out for us and made possible for us to enter. Jesus is the living mystery in whom alone we can discover who we are.

Action, conversation, questions, prayer

Action

Consider and articulate how many-sided is the work of God's Spirit within us.

Conversation and questions

- Pray not to lose the precious sense of expectancy for the more that God will both give to us and ask of us.
- Do we look forward in hope? To lose the sense of a greater future at God's hand is to admit defeat, and to stand still is to slip back!
- Pray to be ready for the more that God has in store for us.
- Give thanks for the constant surprise of God's love.

Prayer

Lord Jesus
You call us to be your witnesses,
Speak to us, enliven our imaginations,
As we find our security in your love and purposes
And share that expectancy and hope
With others.
Amen.

2

Christmas

———•◦•———

Exploring the text

Matthew's birth narrative begins in the same way that the genealogy began. Unfortunately this is masked in the English translation. Matthew 1.1 begins 'a book [or record] of the *genesis* of Jesus the Messiah' and Matthew 1.18 'the *genesis* of Jesus the Messiah took place in this way' (my translation). This indicates that Matthew is doing the same thing in two different ways. The genealogy tells you how we got to this point, that it was the right time for God to act and that Mary fitted well into the story of God's salvation, a story also peopled by Tamar, Rahab, Ruth and Bathsheba. The birth narrative in 1.18–25 tells how this act of salvation took place. Matthew further links the two, reaching in 1.16 the end of the genealogy by mentioning first Joseph, then Mary, then Jesus, and in 1.18 reversing that pattern by mentioning Jesus, then Mary and finally Joseph.

We begin Matthew 1.18, then, clear that this is the time for God to act and that the genealogy has brought us to the moment when it will become clear what his salvific action will be. However, the use of the word genesis, and the many resonances with Moses that we noted in the Introduction, remind us that this may be a new action but it is one that rests on and arises out of what God has done before.

Joseph

Joseph is a largely ephemeral figure in the Gospels. He appears not at all in Mark and as nothing more than the titular father of Jesus in John ('Jesus son of Joseph from Nazareth', John 1.45). In Luke he is a silent foil to Mary. He is the reason they go to Bethlehem for the census but has no speaking part in the narrative. Only in Matthew does Joseph emerge from the shadows at all, and even here he appears only in the birth narratives before melting from view.

We know three key things about Joseph. The first, and most important, is that he was not, according to both Matthew and Luke, Jesus' biological father. Some scholars have argued that the account of virginal conception grew up in response to claims about Jesus' illegitimacy among the Jewish community; in other words that the account of Jesus' conception was a response to his being identified as illegitimate. There is no doubt that there are claims that Jesus was illegitimate, including the specific reference to Jesus being the son of 'Pantera' or 'Pandera'. These claims, however, are all to be found in the Talmud, and date from centuries after even the latest of the Gospels. As a result it seems likely that it is the other way around and that claims of Jesus' illegitimacy are made in direct response to Christian claims about his virginal conception.

The second thing we are told about Joseph is that he was a craftsman (Matthew 13.55). The Greek word is *tekton*, which can be used to refer to a skilled craftsman in any area but was most often used to describe a worker in wood as opposed to a smith or a stonemason. Mark (6.3) also refers to Jesus as a *tekton*, which is where the tradition arose of Jesus' learning his skill in his father's workshop.

The third and final piece of information we have about Joseph is that he was 'just' or 'righteous'. Again the Greek word is important here. The word *dikaios* is most often used to refer to someone who observes the law. In order to understand the logic of verse 19 it might help to sketch out something of the marital law of the time. Betrothal had full legal status and could take place, in Judaism, at the minimum age of 13 for a boy and 12 for a girl. Once the girl was betrothed she stayed at her father's house until the marriage ceremony, which could take place one or more years after the betrothal. Deuteronomy 22.23–27 contains regulations laying down what is to happen when a betrothed girl 'lies' with a man either in the town or in the country. The penalty in both cases is death, but there is a difference. Both shall die if it happens in the town, but only the man if it happens in the country. This implies that in the town the act would be consensual, whereas in the country it would be rape (i.e. a girl could cry out and be rescued in the town but not in the country).

The penalty for such adultery as set out in Deuteronomy was death by stoning, but it is unclear how often this was enacted as a punishment. There is no anecdotal evidence that it happened in the first century, so Joseph's choice was probably either to take Mary to trial so that a jury could decide whether the sex was consensual or rape, or to divorce her quietly without a trial. Matthew suggests that one option would result in shame whereas the other would not. In reality both would result in shame, since Mary would still be pregnant outside marriage, but one would involve public shame and the other a more private kind. So if we return to Joseph's 'justness', the issue was that if he was law-abiding he had to do one or the other (call a trial or divorce her quietly) but that, not wanting to shame her, he took the second course of action.

Dreams and revelation

What changed Joseph's mind was a revelation from God, whereby he discovered that Mary's pregnancy was a result neither of rape nor of consensual sex. As a result his decision not to divorce her meant that he was still 'just'. The revelation occurred in a dream, via an 'angel of the Lord'. Intriguingly, in the Old Testament these two never occur together. Either the angel of the Lord appears (as with Moses at the burning bush, Exodus 3.1–5), or the person concerned has a dream (for example, Joseph in Genesis 28.10–17), but not both. The appearance of both suggests a reinforcement of the revelation's truth. In case anyone was in doubt, an angel of the Lord appeared in a dream.

The revelation itself, however, takes an Old Testament pattern: the announcement of the birth and the revelation of the child's name and identity. Here the angel declares that a child will be born, he will be called Jesus and he will save people from their sins (Matthew 1.21). Let us compare this with the announcement of the birth of Ishmael:

> And the angel of the LORD said to her, 'Now you have conceived and shall bear a son; you shall call him Ishmael, for the LORD has given heed to your affliction. He shall be a wild ass of a man, with his hand against everyone, and everyone's hand against him; and he shall live at odds with all his kin.'
>
> (Genesis 16.11–12)

Or with that of Solomon:

> But the word of the LORD came to me, saying, 'You have shed much blood and have waged great wars; you shall not build a house to my name, because you have shed so much blood in my sight on the earth. See, a son shall be born to you; he shall be a man of peace. I will give him peace from all his enemies on every side; for his name shall be Solomon, and I will give peace and quiet to Israel in his days. He shall build a house for my name. He shall be a son to me, and I will be a father to him, and I will establish his royal throne in Israel forever.'
>
> (1 Chronicles 22.8–10)

If we do so, a very similar pattern emerges. Joseph's revelation was of the type that appeared in the Old Testament and, as a result, served to confirm the impact of the message.

Immanuel and Isaiah 7.14

Matthew's gloss on this episode characteristically contains a reference to prophecy and raises one of the key questions about his use of the Old Testament. Matthew claims that Jesus' birth took place to fulfil a prophecy made by Isaiah. The particular reference cited by Matthew suggests that this is obvious, until we explore the prophecy in more depth. Isaiah 7 was written during a specific conflict in the history of Judah. The southern kingdom of Judah was under threat from its neighbours in the north. Ahaz, who was king at the time, was terrified of the consequences and Isaiah came to see him by the water supply to the city, where he prophesied that Ahaz should not fear and should trust God, and that if he did so all would be well. Isaiah offered him a sign that a young woman would conceive a child and by the time he was weaned (about two years), the threat would be gone. As it happened, Ahaz ignored the prophecy entirely and sent to Assyria for help, an action that eventually led to the destruction of Israel in the north.

Two questions emerge from this account. The first is to do with timing. It is clear that Isaiah's prophecy had already been fulfilled in the eighth century BC, so why would it became an issue again in the first century AD? This taps into a much bigger question of the use of so-called messianic prophecies in the New Testament. If they can be seen already to have been fulfilled before the time, does this mean that they cannot also be used as prophecies of Jesus' birth? Some would say yes to this, but many scholars would argue for the existence of something often called telescopic prophecy, which means that prophecy can be seen to be fulfilled on more than one occasion. It can be true both in its original context and at a much later date. Theologically, if Jesus is seen to be the fulfilment of all God's promises to Israel then, by extension, prophecies of future hope can all be seen to find their fulfilment in him.

A much more contentious issue has often been the word translated in the NRSV as 'young woman' (Isaiah 7.14) but in the ESV as 'virgin' (indeed, one of the motivations behind the ESV was to correct some of these translations, which were perceived to undermine the messianic prophecies). The Hebrew word, *almah*, means a young woman who was 'ripe sexually' and might have been a virgin or a newly married girl. The Greek text used the word *parthenos* to translate the Hebrew word *almah* and this was much more explicitly 'virgin'. In putting the verse into Greek, Matthew used the word that clearly meant 'virgin', not just 'young woman'. Some have argued that this is what led him to provide the details of the virginal conception, though it is not necessary to take this view since Luke also refers to a virginal conception. And the same response can be given to this as to the question of whether the prophecy can refer to Jesus as well as the unknown woman and child during Isaiah's time. If Jesus fulfilled this prophecy uniquely as the one who uniquely fulfilled all God's promises, then this opens the possibility that the use of *parthenos* could be seen to fit Jesus' circumstances in a way they did not fit the original prophecy.

Matthew 1.18–25 brings another feature of Matthew's theology to the fore. The genealogy points to the fact that the time of Jesus was *the* moment for God to act; coupled with this, Matthew 1.18–25 indicates that Jesus fulfilled in a unique way the promises that God had made of salvation. This strand of fulfilment flows onwards through the rest of the Gospel, and through the rest of Matthew's account of Jesus' life.

Imagining the text

Through his respect for Mary and his loving care for her child Jesus, whom he names and accepts as his own, Joseph becomes a model of obedience and practical love. Joseph shows a deep, spiritual, attentive listening to God which is expressed in his faithful cooperation with God's will, even when this defies convention and puts his own honour and reputation at risk. As a husband, father, leader and workman, Joseph shows a profound and secure masculinity – he is a man who listens carefully, trusts his inner convictions, serves others and puts his commitment to the responsibilities of care before any sense of

superior status, desire to make money or fear of what others
will think of him. Like many key figures in Scripture, Joseph's
vision of God's purposes is revealed to him through dreams.
This poem plays with the themes of Joseph as dreamer and
carpenter who is worked upon by God, and works alongside
God in taking forward the history of salvation in Jesus. Joseph
is an encouragement to all disciples of Jesus who must make
difficult choices as to how their deepest inner convictions are to
find priority alongside other commitments.

Joseph dreaming

Like you, I am a maker of things:
in my case rafters, tables, doors and frames,
with their discreet joints holding strain,
dispersing it.
I can price a job, the quantities of required materials,
the cost in energy and time –
how to deliver in three days, in six – then to stand back
   afterwards
for proper rest, to appreciate what is well done
though unacknowledged.
Like anyone who knows their craft
I will see the hidden skill in ordinary things which work.

I am not the first man you have come to
by way of his inner door:
you send your messengers through sleep,
swift artisans of spirit,
each with their task to undertake by morning.
This was your way with wrestling Jacob rested on his desert
   pillow-stone,
with Joseph too in Egypt, vision running free in prison time
unchained across the years,
first seven, then seven more.

Apprenticed to these other dreamers,
I become my own Daniel,
feeling for the grain of purpose
in the unseeing lumber yard of night;
discerning in the darkness
I have listened for your finger
on the latch of my heart,
for the noiseless turning hinge,
your angel stepping through the frame
into a secret chamber beyond mind,
workshop where the character is shaped and honed
to wake re-hung, new strengthened,
schooled by your design, obedient.

As you have spoken without words,
so I have woken time after time to do your will
through gestures,
as any mate would do
labouring for the gaffer expert in his trade.
Exact, and to your specifications
I disregard convention just sufficiently for the job in hand:
first to take the lady,
then her child,
then to forgo home, and business,
to become a foreigner, until the time is right
until another dream slips through to take us further
along your bridge of providence
slung between one divine disruption and the next.

Reflecting on the text

The Christmas message is shared in so many different ways.
Whether we hear the truth in the form of story or in more
abstract words, as we reflect on the text we should try to

combine the simplicity and the wonder of God's gift. It is universal in its scope and purpose.

God's act of love for us

Matthew's narrative shares with us the birth of a new baby. It is the sign of a new beginning: a new hope; light shining in the darkness; the dawning of a new day in the narrative of God's love for us; a new outpouring of love – all this longing and expectation carried in a new life. The story of Bethlehem has endless power because it signifies all these things and more. Let us consider one theme – innocence.

Innocence is poignant because Christmas seems to express a kind of nostalgia for lost innocence. The virgin snow . . . jolly coachmen from the never-never land of Merrie England. Animals. Dear Old Santa Claus with nothing more menacing to say than 'Ho Ho Ho!' Memories of Christmas past when children's eyes shone with excitement and before turkeys looked like frozen footballs wrapped in plastic.

Unforgivable nostalgia. But buried within it a search for lost innocence. A longing for a world as it might have been before it all became so complicated, so murky, so full of tragedy, so unfair and so threatening, so worldly wise.

Innocence. Not ignorance or naivety. In Jesus we see it. Not the kind of innocence to be sheltered, kept out of conflict, untouched by pain and sorrow, blind to the world's evil.

Innocence is part of the truth of Jesus and is a quality that our lives and world are in need of. It is a kind of fierce integrity, an innocent, straightforward relationship with God, an uncluttered moral insight, what the Bible calls 'purity of heart'. And that was how he could go straight to the hearts of those who needed him.

Why do we need this quality? Think of the extraordinary deviousness of much that goes on in life. There is little room for innocence around the negotiating table. The inner reality of our dealings seems often to be a horrendous mixture of bluff and double bluff, suspicion, lies, checks and counter-checks. This is as true of our religious institutions as it is of politics. We seem to be trapped within the dynamics of a profound loss of trust.

Or think of the picture of human deviousness and casual sin fed to us through the media. We are constantly titillated by scandals. We are bombarded by images of a cynical society where innocence is a faintly ludicrous handicap. Yet in our own relationships we are often only too ready to exchange vulnerability and sincerity for the superficiality of chatter, uninformed impression and a lack of compassion and care for others.

Yet – that cannot be all. Christmas can haunt us with the image of a child for whom the angels sing. We cannot escape the challenge of a life which was transparent to God. We cannot turn our backs on the truth that in all the mess and confusion and frightening complexity of life, the love which came down at Christmas still points us to the heart of the matter, the meaning and purpose of life and living. God is at the beating heart of our lives, and we follow Christ, the one who shows us how to be whole.

The innocent eye cannot be recovered by simply wishing for it. We can go in heart and mind to see the babe lying in a manger. We can look to him whose innocence of vision can begin to take hold of ours, who can restore to life a new sanity, direction and strength.

When the shepherds came to Bethlehem they wondered and worshipped.

So please God, shall we. Amen.

Jesus fulfils the promises that God has made of salvation

I have often wondered about those many people who must, for all kinds of reasons, spend Christmas alone. I wonder which words, of the many that fill the Christmas season, might be suited to this context and moment. Salvation, which is sometimes rendered healing, might be something to ponder on and it is certainly a major theme of the Gospel of Matthew.

Healing means wholeness and it is not to be confused with the absence of disease or hurt. Healing is accessible to all. It does not mean perfection, and indeed a life can be far from perfect and still be whole. Indeed, no life can be truly complete unless it includes everything – the good and the bad, the joyful and the sad, the beauty and the ugliness.

The Christmas narrative contains so much. Angels, animals, shepherds, an unmarried mother and an older father, people filled with expectation, hopeful, but also consumed with political cynicism. It is all in the story, and we see it in our lives today. It is the diversity of our world, the confusion of our days, the chaos of ourselves. It is difficult to see the whole because we only see the parts.

I think that religious people are often too good at sorting the good from the bad, the joy from the sadness, the beautiful from the ugly. We sort and separate, control and organize so as not to contaminate. It is as if, on the desks of our lives, we put the perfect on one side and the imperfect on the other.

This is not Matthew's way of drawing us into the story. This is not God's way of dealing with us! It is all drawn together, and we are drawn to it – drawn to the improbably comforting image of that strange, crude diversity huddled around a baby. This incarnates what we know to be true. Life is wild and uncontrollable, unpredictable and gloriously fragile. When we see it all together, we see it whole – healed of our divisions, our categories, our judgements.

Gradually, like our watching the dawn, realisation takes shape in light. We can emerge from the cold, lonely, frightening darkness and see ourselves and our life in a new light.

Whole, as God created it and especially as God nurtures it in love.

Action, conversation, questions, prayer

Action

Let us long to deepen our love of God – for his own sake.

Conversation and questions

- How might we nurture adoration in our discipleship?
- Pray to feel the wonder of God's simplicity of love.
- What are the gifts of God that give you cause for thankfulness?

Prayer

As we gather around the crib,
Come close to us and help us to see
Afresh the mystery of your gift of love
Held, cradled and shared
For our life and healing.
For this we give you thanks and praise.
Amen.

3

Epiphany

—•◆•—

Exploring the text

People often speak of the 'birth narratives' of Matthew, and due to the influence both of Luke's account and of popular renderings of the nativity, it is easy to miss that Matthew has very little in the way of a proper 'birth narrative'. There is material which refers to what happened before Jesus' birth (which we looked at in the previous chapter) and material which refers to what happened after his birth, but very little material relating to his birth per se. Matthew's so-called birth narratives could more accurately be called 'epiphany narratives', in that they focus on first the finding and then the worship of Jesus by the Magi.

The dating of Jesus' birth

So much has been made of the historicity (or lack of it) of the accounts of Jesus' birth that it is important to pause and explore the arguments a little here. The first question, though possibly the least important, is that of the dating of Jesus' birth. As many people know, the key problem here is that Herod the Great, one of the major characters of Matthew's account, died in 4 BC. As a result Jesus' birth must have taken place earlier than the year 0. There has also been extensive discussion of the star which guided the Magi to Bethlehem. The most popular solution is that the star was a comet, and in Chinese astronomy there is reference to a comet or maybe a nova in 5 BC. This pushes some to a date of around 6 to 5 BC.

An additional conundrum is raised not by Matthew's Gospel but by Luke's. Luke claims that a census was the reason Joseph and Mary went to Bethlehem in the first place. The problem here is two-fold. First, there is no evidence that people were required to return to their family's home for a census, and second the closest major census to this period dates, from the records of the Jewish historian Josephus, to around AD 6 to 7. As a result we either have to assume that Luke got his facts muddled or that another, much smaller (and therefore un-recorded) census was held ten years earlier.

Related to the question of dating is the question of Bethlehem as the place where Jesus was born. Much is made by both Luke and Matthew of the fact that Bethlehem was the location of Jesus' birth, though they include slightly different details. Luke believes Nazareth to be Joseph and Mary's home and Bethlehem only a temporary stopping place, whereas Matthew appears to view Bethlehem as their home and the place from which they fled Herod, only to resettle in Nazareth after his death. This points to a double tradition (known by both Matthew and Luke) in which Bethlehem was Jesus' place of birth and Nazareth his place of upbringing. How and why they moved from one to another is probably less important than the fact that both Gospels record a similar tradition on this point.

The historicity of the accounts

Much more important than this is the question of whether the birth narratives have, in fact, been entirely made up by the Gospel writers, pieced together from Old Testament texts to form a tradition. The word 'midrash' is often used to describe such a piecing together. The problem is that it is almost imposs-ible to argue either for or against the historicity of the birth narratives. Definitive proof would require texts outside the New Testament and independent of it to corroborate the evidence of the Gospel writers. Since such evidence does not exist, it is very difficult to argue definitively about the matter.

Arguments in favour of the historicity of the narratives are that, although apparently independent of each other, Matthew's and Luke's basic facts cohere: that Joseph was Jesus' legal but not his biological father; that Mary was his mother and was a virgin at his conception by the Holy Spirit; and that Jesus was born in Bethlehem, whatever the reason for his family being there.

Also suggesting historicity is the role attributed to Herod. The slaughter of the innocents is not recorded anywhere outside the New Testament, but the number of children slaughtered may have been quite small (possibly around 12 to 15) given the probable size of Bethlehem at the time. However, Herod was renowned for his brutal behaviour, having killed his own sons and even his own wife when they threatened his popularity. Herod's real difficulty was that he had no claim to be 'King of the Jews' at all. His family came from Idumea, an area re-annexed into Judea during the time of the Hasmoneans (the descendants of Judas Maccabeus) and so was not considered to be properly Jewish by some of his compatriots, nor was he descended from David or from Judas Maccabeus (though his wife Mariamne was a Hasmonean; it is thought he married her to increase his credibility). Herod was known to be wily, brutal and insecure. He had manipulated the Romans into giving him the title of king, but was always terrified that someone with a better claim to the title might wrest it from him by popular acclaim. Therefore, although there is no evidence he did kill the children, such an action would have been entirely consistent with what is known of him from elsewhere.

Arguments against the historicity of the accounts are that there is very little overlap between Matthew's and Luke's accounts (beyond what has been outlined above) and that the accounts seem to rely heavily on Old Testament sources. So, for example, Jesus' birth in Bethlehem is explained by Matthew's use of a combination of Micah 5.2 and 2 Samuel 5.2, and the slaughter of the infants is associated with the weeping of Rachel over her exiled children in Jeremiah 31.15. There are also hints of Numbers 24.17 ('a star shall come out of Jacob'), Psalm 72.10 ('may the kings of Sheba and Seba bring gifts'), and Isaiah 60.3 ('Nations shall come to your light, and kings to the brightness of your dawn') and 60.6 ('they shall bring gold and frankincense, and shall proclaim the praise of the LORD'). Indeed the references from Psalm 72.10 and Isaiah 60.3 are probably the reason that the Magi became associated with kings in Christian tradition. Add to all of this the strong parallels between the events that took place around Jesus' birth and that of Moses (the mention of Egypt; that a wicked king – Pharaoh/Herod – tried to kill them at birth; that other babies died at the same time; etc.) and you can begin to see why people make the case that the birth narratives were a creative stitching together of Old Testament tradition.

However, it is important to recognize why Matthew makes this strong connection between Jesus and Old Testament tradition. In the previous chapter, we made reference to telescopic prophecy (see p. 28). Here we need to take this one step further. One of the striking features that emerges from a reading of the Old Testament is that some of the key events seem blurred together. The best example of this can be found in Psalm 74.12–13, 'Yet God my King is from of old, working salvation in the earth. You divided the sea by your might.' A first reading of this might suggest that the Psalmist is referring to the parting of the Red Sea at the Exodus, but the next phrase, 'you broke the heads of the dragons in the waters', rather confuses that. It becomes clear that God's act of salvation at creation and the Exodus have been combined in this reference. They are, to all intents and purposes, the same event. What this means is that the writers of the Old Testament saw God's acts of salvation happening again and again and again and interpreted them as the same event being repeated in a slightly different form.

It seems that Matthew may have been doing the same thing here. His eclectic gathering of references from around the

Old Testament all serve to prove that God's age-old acts of salvation – creation, the Exodus, the settling in the Land, the return from exile, etc. – are being repeated, perfectly and wholly, in the birth of Jesus. Jesus' birth marks a new creation, the coming of a new Moses and a new David, a new Exodus and a return from exile. Jesus' birth *is* the same act of salvation happening again, only this time in a perfect fulfilment of all that God has promised. To interpret Matthew's account solely in terms of a stitching together of Old Testament traditions is to miss the point of what he was doing here.

Worship by the Magi

Very little is known about the Magi. The Greek word 'Magi' originally referred to a caste of Persian priests renowned for their ability to interpret dreams. However, their association in Matthew with astrology might suggest a connection with Babylon, where astrology was much more popular. Then again, the gifts that they brought suggest a closer association with Arabia or the Syrian Desert. All of this suggests that the term Magi was used loosely to describe a group (of unknown number) from the East who came bringing Eastern gifts. The key thing that we should not overlook is the importance for Matthew of what they do when they arrive.

Matthew 2.11 says that when they found Jesus, the Magi 'paid him homage' (NRSV) or 'worshipped him' (NIV). It is important here to keep 'worship' in the text, since the word becomes important again at the end of the Gospel. In the Great Commission in Matthew 28.16–20 the disciples also worship (the same Greek word is used here) the risen Jesus and then are sent outwards to make disciples of all nations. This most Jewish of Gospels reminds us that, in fact, the first people to worship Jesus in the first place were Gentiles from unknown nations beyond Israel's borders. At Jesus' birth the Magi travelled many miles to worship Jesus; now the disciples are to travel to ensure that more Gentiles can do the same.

Imagining the text

This poem celebrates the perseverance and patience of Joseph – carpenter, husband of Mary and guardian of Jesus. With persistent obedience and care he takes on each tricky task in fulfilling his role in the story of Jesus: accepting that Mary's pregnancy is part of God's plan, flouting convention to take her as his wife, caring for the child Jesus as God's Messiah in ways which demand from him great courage, initiative and flexibility – guiding the family to safety in Egypt, living there as refugees, and then settling to practise his trade in unfamiliar Galilee. All this shows model character and skill which makes a major contribution to God's 'renovation project' of salvation for a world in need of healing and renewal.

The house that Joseph built

I took on an awkward job once,
to mend a clumsy house – I swear it had a squint
and broken back:
walls askew, angles in an argument,
almost every part of it untrue, at odds,
going to ruin.

Make it beautiful he said,
Make it elegant he said,
Make it fit for a bride he said,
  upon her honeymoon.

To make it work
I had to love that property;
each quirk and fault
I valued like my own design;
each defect fixed with splice and peg
and blended wood, as if I'd always meant it.

Make it warm he said,
Make it comfortable he said,
Make it dry and safe enough he said,
   for a mother and her baby.

It taught me, this dumb house,
that being a craftsman is sometimes to embrace
the un-chosen task
and the failings of others,
to bring a generous expertise
which mends, and makes a future.

Make it broad he said,
Make it tall he said,
Make it big enough he said,
   for visitors to come and wonder.

Make it calm he said,
Make it still he said,
Make it cool he said,
   for a corpse to sleep his way through Sabbath.

Reflecting on the text

The Epiphany brings us all into conversation

Reading and attending to Scripture is a constant adventure, strewn as it is with wonderful phrases of multiple meaning. Look again at the familiar reference to the Magi, who 'having been warned in a dream not to return to Herod, they left their country by another road'. What do we see in this? Perhaps the political acumen of the Magi certifies their wisdom? But perhaps we also remember that nearly everyone who encounters Jesus ends up going home another way. The encounter with Jesus changes people, makes them different. After they have met this

Jesus, they seem incapable – or certainly unwilling – to go back the same way they came.

The feast of the Epiphany and the season that follows is, for the Church, traditionally one of mission and evangelism. Of course, for the modern Church, there are very few mission fields available, few places where the basic outlines of the gospel have not penetrated geographical, political and cultural barriers in one fashion or another. And evangelism demands some good news to proclaim, but on too many days there seems precious little good to report. Yet there is still a right mission field remaining for all of us if only we turn our sights inward.

If we look around the manger, if we look at those who surrounded Jesus throughout his life, and even at those who stood about him at his death, we find that they were as diverse a lot as one might find. Like us. For if truth be told, when you get right down to it, we probably do not have much in common, you and I; the only thing we have in common is this person, Jesus. And that is certainly true for those of us who gather around a shared table. Even when we cannot agree on what Jesus looked like, or what he thought, or the meaning of what he said and did, we can still acknowledge that he is our common connection.

That was his singular gift – a genuine gift, something inherent in his person, and not some skill he crafted or strategy he employed. On the first Epiphany he was but an infant. Yet the force of this person was such that the different gathered around him. And, as people will, no doubt they talked. They engaged in conversation. They talked over the baby, I imagine. About many things. Where they had come from. Where they were. And it was all as much a mystery to them as it is to us.

Reflecting upon Epiphany and the journey of the Magi I wonder if Jesus' primary ministry – his most practical ministry – is that he brought, and continues to bring, people into conversation with one another. Away from our respective tasks and out of our exclusive differences, he puts us in conversation with one another. He calls us and encourages us in that most intimate and dangerous activity, which is conversation. For to be in conversation is to be in the midst of change.

Every time I open my mouth, I risk revealing something of myself that can change me or the world around me. And every time I open myself to receive what another says, I run the risk of being changed by what that person says. God knows how many times my heart, my mind, my life has been changed by the power of another's words shared in conversation. Is it any wonder that so many of us recoil from this dangerous activity, retreat into ourselves?

Yet here we are, and in many other times and places, gathered for the express purpose of conversation. Perhaps with God; certainly with that spirit and power of God that is manifested in what passes between us and among us. We are here, drawn like the Magi by this compelling person who is Jesus. We are here with Jesus, and with one another, perhaps to grow a little more wise, and definitely to return home by a different way.

Holy Innocents

We might wonder why Herod had good cause to fear the children. Is it possible to understand in Herod's fear of children something that is human and tragically manifested in so many ways?

The new, unwed or ill-prepared mother who abandons her newborn baby is not a freak. She is frightened. A baby is an overwhelming responsibility, a living, breathing, profound and ultimate dependency. Nurtured as we are in fierce independence, it is a wonder we admit children into our lives at all. Little surprise that so many are literal accidents, or are treated as accessories. If we pause only for a moment to admit fully into ourselves the import of creating another human life, we find ourselves at the imposing threshold of mystery, where fear begins. Once, it was all we needed for birth control, sufficient to rein in passion and temper judgement.

Children are a raw possibility. They may become anything. They are living icons not only of our innocence and vulnerability, but of our undisciplined egotism and unbridled emotions. Yes, they can be tender and sweet and endearing and achingly touching. But they can be immovably centred on themselves and their way. A child can wound with a word, can dismember a beloved toy or destroy a treasured heirloom, can pierce the air with incessant cries regardless of the hour. A child's frame can contain a raging force so strong that an adult is scarce able to pin it to the ground – ask any schoolteacher.

Children can fill us with pride or take our lives. They are complex and unpredictable. Is that precocious intellect or an intimation of sinister malevolence? Is that hair, those clothes, that jewellery and make-up evidence of creative originality or sociopathy? Is that a sophisticated science project in that box or will I learn later today that my child has blown up the school?

One never knows with a child. One never knows what might be coming. So, with this picture in mind, we might understand why Herod was frightened, why he ordered the children to be killed. All of them for the sake of the one, the one who would eventually die for them all. The one who reminds us that God's incarnation as a child is not simply evidence of God's ultimate dependency but also of God's eternal unpredictability, God's raw possibility. The death of the holy innocents, and the death of the holy innocence – the naive assumption that dares to look upon the child in the manger without fear.

Action, conversation, questions, prayer

Action

Consider resolving to listen more closely to others and what they have to share, especially those who differ from us and those with whom we disagree.

45

Conversation and questions

- Reflect on the beautiful simplicity of Christ to be venerated even by those of complex and sophisticated minds.
- Consider the simple wonder of the role Jesus plays on God's behalf.
- What do we mean by innocence? How might our lives reflect this quality?
- It is hard to be truly universal in spirit and in the welcome we extend to others. Pray for openness of heart.
- Are you excited by your faith?

Prayer

Creator God,
Lift our horizons
Beyond the narrowness of our self-preoccupation
To the gift and adventure of faith
That deepens our sensitivities
And gives us cause to share
Your love every day
In the name of Jesus.
Amen.

4

The Sundays before Lent

Exploring the text

The readings for the Sundays before Lent are, with one exception, taken from the first of Matthew's five narratives and discourses, which we noted in the Introduction to this book (see pp. 7–8). In fact, they are taken from the most famous discourse of all – the Sermon on the Mount. Here we find most clearly Matthew's vision of Jesus as the new Moses giving the new law.

So much has been written on the Sermon on the Mount that it is very difficult to find anything new or interesting to say about it. Nevertheless a few introductory comments may be useful.

The Sermon on the Mount

The first thing to notice is that this most famous of sermons is almost certainly misnamed. As a 'sermon' it simply does not hang together as a piece of teaching. Indeed, if any modern sermon were to be preached in this kind of style (a long string of aphorisms and apparently disconnected themes) or structure (of which there is little to be found), then the preacher would rightly be castigated by her hearers. This points us to the fact that, though these are probably Jesus' own words, Matthew has gathered them together here (as he has also done four times elsewhere, in chapters 10, 13, 18 and 24—25) to provide a significant block of teaching. Indeed, if any one thing could be said to be characteristic of Jesus in Matthew, it would be that

47

in Matthew Jesus' teaching is not, as in Mark, sprinkled through his everyday activities, but expounded in serious and significant blocks. Here Jesus is clearly a rabbi providing teaching to his followers.

Although there is no clear structure to the Sermon on the Mount (as evidenced by the fact that almost every commentator proposes a slightly different one), the first part of the sermon does have some kind of form and direction. Matthew 5.1—6.18 reflects on the question of what living faithfully in the kingdom might look like. It begins with the Beatitudes, which at first appear to be classic wisdom sayings such as might be found in the Old Testament, e.g. 'Blessed/happy are those who do not follow the advice of the wicked' (Psalm 1.1). The key difference, however, is the timing of the reward. The wisdom sayings of the Old Testament all promise a reward in the present, whereas the Beatitudes look much further into the future for their hope of fulfilment. In other words, Jesus encourages his followers to look beyond the present and to recognize that lack of reward does not mean a failure of promise.

Following the Beatitudes comes some significant teaching on the relationship between the Jesus community and the law: Jesus did not abolish the law but came to fulfil it (5.17). The six antitheses, as they are called – 'You have heard that it was said . . . but I say to you' (5.21–48) – offer six illustrations of the way in which this fulfilment works itself out in everyday life. In some ways Jesus sets himself up here as the 'antithesis' of the Pharisees. The Pharisees' major concern was the minutiae of how the law was worked out in practice; the six antitheses are not concerned with the minutiae of practice but with the principle that lies behind the Torah. Here, as in many places in Matthew's Gospel, it is possible to discern a fundamental disagreement between two communities about what faithful following of the law looked like. The Pharisees argued that it involved ever closer detail; Jesus that close detail often meant you missed what the law was really saying. Time and time again in Matthew, Jesus draws his hearers back to the internal disposition that you need in order to follow the law properly, rather than the external action demanded, an internal disposition that often asks far more of the follower than 'just' carrying out what the law commands.

Many people have disputed whether the summary of the law (e.g. Matthew 22.39; Mark 12.31; Luke 10.27) came from Jesus or not. Most scholars today would accept that it was a common summary that was well known in first-century Judaism. Implicit additional support for this view can be found in the Sermon on the Mount. The six antitheses focus on the part of the summary concerned with loving your neighbour, and are followed at the beginning of chapter 6 (1–18) with commands about piety, or the practice of the worship of God. Jesus' illustration of his fulfilment of the law involved first love of neighbour and then love of God. Again the three acts of piety (6.1–8) are illustrative of the kind of attitude a faithful follower of the law might adopt. These are followed by teaching on prayer (6.9–13) and on forgiveness of sins (6.14–15).

It is at 6.18 that any semblance of structure in the Sermon on the Mount breaks down. Matthew 6.19—7.12 contains what most commentators call 'Other Teachings', a succession of important, if apparently unconnected, teachings on subjects ranging from attitudes to money to judgement of one's neighbour. Clarity only really returns in 7.13–29, in which teaching on judgement is combined with an explanation of how to recognize the two different kinds of people who will both be judged. In a way 7.13–29 summarizes the key parts of the rest of the Sermon on the Mount, drawing together the theme of future judgement encountered in the Beatitudes with the acknowledgement that inner disposition produces fruit and that the nature of someone's inner disposition can be recognized by the fruit it bears.

The Sermon on the Mount, then, has discernible themes but no overall structure – especially in the central section, 6.19—7.12,

where a wide range of apparently unconnected themes are
treated together.

Six mountains

We cannot leave the Sermon on the Mount, however, without
noticing another of Matthew's great themes: that of mountains.
Here we need to be clear that the patterns readers observe in
a text are simply that – observable patterns – and nothing more.
The reason for emphasizing this here is that mountains play
an important part in Matthew's Gospel, and it is therefore
tempting to try to impose Matthew's love of fives (and even
the five sections into which the Gospel may be divided) on
to these mountains. Indeed some scholars have gone to great
lengths to weave together Matthew's five sections with the
mountain theme. The problem is that it simply does not go:
there are six mountains in Matthew, not five, and the only way
to ensure a match is to omit or ignore one.

Nevertheless the six mountains are intriguing, since something important always happens on a mountain in Matthew.
The first mountain is the mountain of temptation (Matthew
4.8), on which Jesus is tempted to worship the devil. In Luke
Jesus is simply taken 'up', but here the invitation to worship
is made specifically on a mountain. This is followed in 5.1 with
the Sermon on the Mount(ain); the parallel sermon in Luke
takes place on a plain. The third mountain is where Jesus heals
many sick people (15.29), and the fourth is the mountain of
transfiguration (17.1). The fifth mountain is the Mount of
Olives, where Jesus teaches his disciples about the signs of the
end, and the sixth the mountain where he meets the disciples
after his resurrection (28.16) for the Great Commission. It
is almost as though the six mountains provide a summary of
Jesus' ministry in Matthew: resistance to temptation, teaching,
healing, transfiguration, teaching about the end and commis-
sioning. These six, whether intentionally or not, offer us a clear
introduction to the Jesus of Matthew's Gospel.

Imagining the text

Taking the idea of a five-fold structure for Matthew's Gospel which mirrors the five-volume structure of the Torah, and describes the identity of Jesus in terms of Moses, Israel's great teacher and the leader of his enslaved people to freedom in God's promised land, this poem follows the route of the first unit, which features in Matthew 3 — 7. This unit begins with Jesus' baptism by John in the river Jordan, his sojourn for 40 days in the wilderness, his calling of the first disciples to leave their nets and follow him, his powerful teaching, and his healing of the many distressed individuals brought to him by the great crowds who come to him in Galilee (3.1 — 4.25). Then Jesus ascends the mountain and gives the Sermon on the Mount, teaching the values and conduct of the kingdom of God (5.1 — 7.27), compelling teaching which restores the authority of Israel's religion in the hearts and minds of the people (7.28 – 29).

This narrative flow resonates with the Exodus story: God's chosen servant Moses leading Israel through the Red Sea, the journey through the wilderness for 40 years in which Israel is tested and Moses calls others to share in his leadership and governance of the people, a journey in which God gives him the law and he teaches the people how to live in holiness, justice and mercy, fulfilling the covenant relationship which is to characterize the corporate life of redeemed Israel in the promised land. Those who respond to Jesus' call in every age undergo the same journey, becoming his disciples through baptism, incorporated into the new Israel of the Church, learning to know their need of God's mercy and to seek God's kingdom by living lives of radical trust, compassion and practical love. The leap of imagination implied by Jesus' image of God's kingdom invites his disciples to transform their understanding of present troubles and uncertainties through trust and hope in God's rule and abiding presence among them.

New Exodus

If you will make this journey with me,
travelling is to follow
first through water into
thirst; to leave behind familiar country
then to find your own hunger
in another's need for cure,
walking with the undesired
as company, side by side
together searching out the land of promise which
requires of you one toll to pass
into its sweet ecology
where kindness flourishes:
love is the law and language, love the labour, tax and
the reward of every day eternal living in this gifted place.

Reflecting on the text

Learning to be happy?

On these remote hills above Lake Galilee, Jesus was going to teach his newly called twelve disciples his fundamental lessons about life with God. What did Jesus teach his newly called twelve? Did Jesus teach his inner core of beliefs? Did he teach them about prayer? About Bible reading? About love and justice? No. Jesus began with something much more basic and simple. Jesus began by teaching his newly called disciples about ... happiness, the simplicities of happiness.

All people are interested in happiness. We all want to be happy. Rich and poor, young and old, male and female, we long to experience happiness. We all want it, look for it, and try to find it.

There is an Arabic proverb that says, 'All sunshine and no rain makes for a desert.' I have found that to be true: All sunshine in life and no rain in life makes for a desert. Karl Barth, the famous theologian, said, 'A generation that has no great anguish in its heart will have no great music on its lips.' It is equally true. Great music and great art are born in times of anguish and adversity. Great hearts are *only* born in times of adversity and anguish.

Happiness is different things to different people. Here are some questions that might focus what happiness means for us.

'What are some of the happiest moments in your life?' Think back to the times when you were enormously happy. Can you recall such moments? It may have been your wedding day, or the birth of a baby, or an experience of making a difference in your community.

Here is another question: 'What *places* make you the happiest?' Not the people but the places. What are the places that create an inner smile inside you? For some of you, it may be when you are in your garden, with your fingers in the soil, planting seeds and watching flowers grow. For some of you it is being in the mountains: climbing, skiing, seeing the views. For others, the place is your home and you are watching TV. It may be where your grandchildren are; many people have told me it is wherever the grandkids are. For others it is the kitchen, preparing a meal, sitting around the table with your family, the smell of freshly baked bread in the air.

I have another question: 'What are the ingredients that help you to be a happy person?' What things or qualities enable you to be happier and not sadder? Food? Family? Friends? Health? Clothing? Good relationships? A roof over your head? Money in the bank? Knowing that you are loved? All of these? Some of these? What are the ingredients that create a recipe of happiness for you?

Here is a story from the Buddhist tradition. There was a young man who wanted to discover the way to truth, goodness and salvation. The young man came to Buddha and asked him to show him the way to salvation. Buddha took the young man down to the river and out into the middle where the water was waist deep. Buddha took the young man by the back of the neck and pushed his head under water. The young man thought, 'I am being baptized and Buddha will lift up my head shortly.' But Buddha held his head under the water longer and longer. The young man struggled and pushed his head up, but Buddha used both arms and hands and pushed harder and harder on the man's head. Buddha's arms and hands were enormously powerful and strong. The young man tried to force his neck and head up above the water, but Buddha wouldn't let him. The young man was choking under water and Buddha finally let him up. The young man gasped for air and coughed out his words: 'Buddha, why did you do that?' Buddha replied, 'When you thought that you were drowning, what did you desire most?' The young man said, 'Air.' Buddha said, 'When you crave God's goodness and wholeness as much as you craved the air.'

Perhaps when we reflect on the shape of our inner living – the force of what we desire – then might we have a richer and more honest view of what makes us happy?

How to be good?

Writers down the centuries have so very often struggled with what might enable human beings to be good. For some the Beatitudes are moral exhortations. One's actions and attitudes are to be orientated towards the actions and attitudes in these few verses of Matthew 5. It follows that God's people should be meek, should show mercy. And so we are encouraged to see the Christian life as an ideal to be pursued, our moral maxim.

There are very obvious difficulties in this approach, for all of us fall short. It may be, as we read this passage, that we have a sense that the promised blessing continues to be elusive both in our own personal lives and the life of the wider society, and indeed, especially within our religious communities. Can any of us ever achieve what the text apparently demands?

There is another approach to the Beatitude that recognizes that it is first and foremost a blessing promised by God to those who already are what the Beatitude describes. So the meek, those who mourn and the merciful, can hear the text as a word of encouragement and reassurance. In their predicament they are named by God for blessing and in this might be renewed in hope for the future. This passage should encourage us all to have as part of our commitment to following Christ a deep and passionate longing for the establishment of justice. Within this passage we see a tension between the present and the future – and while we look forward to the completion of God's promise and blessing, the Beatitudes carry a measure of realization in the present.

Matthew reminds us that the Beatitudes are a picture of the direction of God's blessing. God is a God who cares for the poor in spirit, the humble, those yearning for right to be done, the merciful, the single-minded, the peacemakers, and those persecuted for righteousness' sake. God will never abandon them or leave them hopeless. There are, of course, ethical implications for those of us who attend to this text. Our attitudes and consciousness should be shaped by the nature of the God in whom we believe. We are not offered a strategy, but instead some powerful words to enliven our imagination and reform our sensitivities.

Action, conversation, questions, prayer

Action

How do you or your community express the gospel through some aspect of social engagement or action?

Conversation and questions

- How does God shape our attitudes?
- Consider someone in your life who you admire – what makes that person good? How might we learn from the example of others?

- Place before God your deepest desires and cravings – keep in touch with what you long for.
- What are the ingredients that help you to be a happy person?

Prayer

Lord Jesus,
Take my hands and ears and eyes,
Take my mind and heart,
And use them for blessing,
As channels for peace and justice,
Mercy and truth,
In the service of your gospel.
Amen.

5

Lent

———•◦•———

Exploring the text

The Lectionary provides us with slim pickings from Matthew during Lent, since during Lent most of the Gospel readings are from John. This gives us time, therefore, to reflect more deeply on the story of Jesus' temptation in Matthew.

The wilderness wanderings

In both Matthew's and Luke's Gospels it is clear that the temptation narratives draw us back to the wilderness wanderings. Both writers identify the place where Jesus was tested simply as the 'wilderness', the word used in the Septuagint to describe where God's people went after they fled from Egypt. This point is further emphasized by the fact that, in response to the devil's questioning, Jesus quotes three times from Deuteronomy 6—8 and in doing so overturns the people's responses to God during their time in the wilderness. Jesus, unlike them, saw that there was more to living than earthly food (Matthew 4.4; Deuteronomy 8.3), that it was wrong to put God to the test (Matthew 4.7; Deuteronomy 6.16), and that you should worship only God (Matthew 4.10; Deuteronomy 6.13). For more on the temptation narratives as a repetition and reversal of the wilderness wanderings, see the chapter on Lent in *Journeying with Luke* (SPCK, 2012).

If you are the Son of God . . .

It is important to recognize, however, that the temptations are not solely cast as types of the temptation of Israel; they

57

are clearly defined as genuine temptations of Jesus too. This becomes especially apparent in the first two temptations, which the devil prefaces with 'If you are the Son of God . . .' The temptations, then, become questions of how Jesus conceives of his ministry as Son of God. The implication is clearly that he could have chosen his role as Son of God to involve primarily impressive, miraculous acts that nourish only the body, or spectacular deeds backed up by God that easily demonstrate who Jesus really is. However, Jesus has resisted both of these choices. Jesus, of course, did do miracles: some of these miracles fed or healed human bodies; others (like the stilling of the storm) were as spectacular as throwing yourself off a high pinnacle. What the temptation narratives do is to focus our attention on what Jesus' miracles did and did not achieve. The devil was offering Jesus a short-cut to glory and Jesus resisted it. Jesus did not see the miracles as an easy way to notoriety or to proving that he was the Son of God. He did not use the miracles to prove a point about who he was; the miracles flowed out of him *because* he was who he was. In the temptations, and throughout his ministry, Jesus refused to use them as the easy short-cut they could so easily have been.

The reason for this can be seen in the final temptation, where the devil invites Jesus to worship him. This reveals what lies behind the other two temptations: the desire to shift the focus from God onto something else. If Jesus had capitulated to the temptation to use miracles as a proof of who he was, he would have been using them not to point people to the true nature of God but to himself. The aim of all the temptations was to draw the focus away from God.

This is an important theme in Lent. We live in a world in which so many things compete for a place at the centre of our lives. Many of them are, in and of themselves, benign. Just as there is nothing wrong, per se, with turning stones to bread, there is nothing wrong with many of the things that seek a central place in our lives. The only problem is that they are not God. They invite us to put something else in the place where God should be. The season of Lent invites us to spend time, as Jesus did in the wilderness, ensuring that God is to be found at the very centre of our lives, our actions, our motivations. Lent is the season in which we should interrogate our innermost selves, asking whether our own glory, our desire for easy solutions, even our own guilt and remorse, has in fact displaced God from the place where he should be – at the heart of all things.

All the kingdoms of the world

The irony of the temptation narratives comes to the fore in the final temptation in Matthew's Gospel, where the devil offers Jesus 'all the kingdoms of the world and their splendour' (Matthew 4.8) if only he will worship him. Matthew ensures that we do not miss the irony by including both the visit of the Magi (2.11) and Jesus' resurrection account (28.17–18) in the Gospel.

The devil offered Jesus possession of 'all the kingdoms of the world and their splendour'. Whereas we, the readers, know that the representatives of some of those kingdoms have just come to worship Jesus of their own volition, bearing some of their splendour with them. Likewise, at the end of his ministry, Jesus, now in receipt of all authority in heaven and on earth, sends his disciples not to grasp hold of the kingdoms of the world but to offer them a gift, the gift of the good news of Jesus Christ. The third temptation suggests to Jesus another path of being 'Son of God', one which involves taking rather than giving, superficial deeds of power rather than hard-won, sacrificial self-offering. In the third temptation, the devil offers Jesus a short-cut to success which will avoid the pain and cost of being the Son of God on earth, but which also involves grasping what is not his, rather than receiving it freely.

During his temptation in the wilderness, Jesus learned to discern for himself what living out his role as 'Son of God' would entail for him. As a result, Lent also becomes the time when each of us is called to take a similar journey, into the discovery of what living authentically as ourselves with God at the centre of all things might look and feel like.

Imagining the text

In Matthew the desert is a place of testing and of triumph. Like Moses and the people of Israel, journeying through the wilderness for 40 years in which their faith and obedience is tested, Jesus endures temptation and struggle. He is victorious over Satan – he is the obedient Son who fulfils the will of the Father – and his dependence on God is a model for all who seek to follow him as children of the new Israel inaugurated by his life, death and resurrection. The 40-day Lenten journey is an opportunity to repent, to draw closer to God and to amend our lives according to the pattern of Jesus, rooted in God's grace – an extended time for spiritual renewal, seeking closeness to God and our neighbour through prayer, study and self-examination.

These simple limericks invite us to make Lent an opportunity to entertain the spiritual challenges which Jesus makes to us as his disciples: his teaching in Matthew 6 on right conduct in almsgiving, prayer and fasting (readings for Ash Wednesday); and his own journey through the wilderness, recounted in Matthew 4.1–11 (Lent 1). These readings offer us a vision of Lent as a creative space of spiritual renewal rather than a period of moral and ethical turmoil.

When you give alms . . .

Beware benefactors from Barnet
who make much ado with their trumpet:
each generous donation
a standing ovation
for self, not for God who inspires it.

When you pray . . .
Steer clear of the pious from Preston
who litanize only with robes on:
best pray in the buff,
relinquish all stuff
which distracts from who you've set your heart on.

When you fast . . .
Don't look sad like clients of clinics
who diet, celebs just to mimic:
let joy deep inside
feed smiles broad and wide
that brighten the gloom of the cynics.

In the wilderness . . .
God's playful Spirit drives to the wild
a person, a people reconciled,
in a secret place
which offers them space
to be loved and enjoyed, like a child.

Discerning every word that comes from the mouth
of God . . .
In matters concerning the Bible
the tempter likes minds that are idle:
his textual quotations
for harsh disputations
sheer pleasure, if wounding and spiteful.

Forty days and forty nights . . .

The days of temptation are forty,
enough time to be really naughty;
wealth, status and pow'r
are yours in an hour:
fast food for the spiritually haughty.

Then the devil left him . . .

The height of temptation: a mountain;
the depth of renewal: a fountain
which angels release:
unseen days of peace.
Then come crowd, crown and cross, torn curtain.

Reflecting on the text

Matthew 4.1–11: Jesus triumphs over the natural temptations of his mission and (unlike Adam and Eve) is not turned away from what he must be and do.

At the heart of this particular reading, as we begin our journey through Lent, lies a promise and a challenge. The promise is that God is gracious and self-giving, and it lies at the heart of our constant living out, nurturing and expressing the extra-ordinary reality of God's love for us. We are precious and made in his image as we attend to Scripture. The challenge is that, in our search for God, we must let go of our illusions and fantasies. St Paul constantly warns us that living in a world of illusions is both persuasive and destructive. In this season of Lent we might consider the illusions that hinder us in our understanding of God and find expression through our practice of religion.

In the playful poetry above, we are encouraged to use Lent as a creative time, following Jesus into the wilderness and desert, where like him we might ponder who we are and what the shape of our discipleship might take.

One of the difficulties with Lent is the great array of temptations it brings us to give up: to give up on whatever Lenten disciplines, maybe, we have chosen, to give up and so be conscious of failure. Indeed, we sometimes see the whole purpose of Lent as a kind of test of our resolve to stick to our good resolutions. From this perspective, Lent may look like a six-week obstacle course of spiritual and physical challenges to be mastered or endured, so that we may prove to ourselves, to others and to God how strong we are by coming through the ordeal unscathed by failure and having triumphantly resisted the temptation to give in. Such a view of Lent is problematic and full of the danger of spiritual pride – this attempt to be better can become a celebration of our ability and strength rather than anything about the working of God's grace in us.

As we read this Gospel again, let us see Lent differently. It is not about a test or a challenge, and it is certainly not about resisting our own temptation to give in to our weaker natures.

In the struggle of Jesus in the wilderness, and particularly with some core temptations, we are offered wisdom for our own spiritual journey. First, we should ask ourselves what the foundation stones of our trust look like. In other words, in what or whom do we trust? Are we listening to what God might want from us? Have we become stale and unimaginative in venturing out into new and different ways of following Christ? How much do we listen to what God's intentions might be for us?

The devil's first temptation, that Jesus should turn stones into bread is, in effect, a temptation for us to give people what they want. The Church, when she is being faithful and effective, knows that she must be about the meeting of need. Feeding the hungry, binding up the broken and embracing the outcast are vital and central aspects of our discipleship. We might glimpse here God's basic goodwill towards us and safeguard against our own self-reliance as a fantasy! Sometimes the Church needs to be ready to give people what they do not want, to say what we do not want to hear, to ask difficult questions which many might prefer to leave unasked. We might want to explore how we may rely less on the self and more on God, and indeed whether there are unmet needs in ourselves which are preventing us from growing in grace and love.

This points again to the complexity of our inner motivations and intentions. Individuals and communities have attempted to manipulate God into a being who conveniently does and is what we need and want. Put another way, many of us want God on our terms; we overlook some of the radical challenges and demands put on us by the gospel. Perhaps we are being asked to consider the nature of our obedience to God and our inspiration to see in Jesus openness and trust, which generate a generosity of spirit that allows God to be God.

In the third temptation we hear the devil urging Jesus to play the religious card, to reveal his divine status and power by flinging himself from the pinnacle of the Temple and waiting for the angels to save him. The temptation to retreat into holiness and away from the rough and tumble of ordinary worldly existence is always a temptation for us Christians, and it is one that we need to be on our guard against.

We may be tempted to see the world, with its concerns about justice and power, its institutions and tensions, its diversity and divisions, as a passing, transient thing, for we are Godly people destined for heaven, which is somewhere well removed. We should certainly be reminded that the whole world is God's concern. The way we manage society, embrace difference, include all sorts of voices and viewpoints, give honour to strangers and the marginalized – all of this matters, even to the extent of affecting the way we shape and reshape some of our most precious traditions.

Of course Lent is about the biscuit tin, the extra bit of kindness or witness, the study group, a renewed determination in prayer and worship. But attending to this passage of Scripture

reminds us that it is more – much more. Renewal and challenge
of the Church and ourselves, with its discomfort and awkward-
ness, is part of the Lenten wilderness journey. This is a time to
reflect on the powerful human instincts – like wanting to give
people what they want, relying on long trusted but unchallenged
political systems, or retreating into a religious ghetto that is
apparently perfect, but dangerously disconnected from our
world – that are deeply entrenched in our thinking and spiritual
complacency. Lent challenges us to challenge them, as Jesus did
the tempter in his wilderness experience. It will not be comfortable, but it has the potential to give us life and spiritual health.

Action, conversion, questions, prayer

Action
Consider the ways in which you listen to God.

Conversation and questions
- Are we prepared to give whatever it costs to make the commit-
ment that leads to spiritual wisdom and maturity?
- The fact that we are flawed must be humbly accepted if ever
we are to be healed.
- Healing comes from God – can we grasp it gladly?
- Temptations are often minor, but they can be symptoms of
(and the test of) where we really stand.

Prayer
God of the wilderness,
Lead us to face truth, exposed and unprotected;
In times of trial,
Help us to resist
The worship of empty power
And the illusion of invulnerability,
In Jesus Christ, the broken bread.
Amen.

6

Passiontide

———•◦•———

Exploring the text

In Matthew, as in all the Gospels, the climax of the story of Jesus can be found in the last week of his life, in the sweep from the entry into Jerusalem to the crucifixion. As Jesus moves through this last week, the themes of the five narratives and discourses in chapters 1—20 become woven together as he faces the reality of what living out being the 'Son of God' will mean for him. The inevitability of Jesus' death becomes clearer and clearer as we travel through his final week, until in three scenes of chapter 26, it becomes a certainty.

The plot to kill Jesus gains momentum from three key events. The first is Jesus' decision to celebrate the Passover in Jerusalem (26.1–5), the second the anointing of Jesus' feet by the unnamed woman (26.6–13) and the third the visit of Judas to the chief priests (26.14–16). Jesus' decision to come to Jerusalem for the Passover gives his enemies the opportunity to kill him; the anointing of Jesus' feet tips Judas into such anger that he decides to betray him; and Judas' visit to the Jewish authorities provides the means of Jesus' arrest. As a result, the Last Supper takes place in the context of certainty that Jesus is going to die and that this will be his last meal with his disciples.

The Last Supper

Although John's Gospel separates the Last Supper from the Passover meal, Matthew like the other Synoptic Gospels is clear that this is Jesus' last Passover meal with his disciples. Whether it was in fact the Passover meal is at least debatable. If the Last Supper was the Passover meal, then the festival had already begun when Jesus was arrested and tried. The restrictions of Jewish law (coupled with the leaders' decision not to arrest Jesus during the festival; see Matthew 26.5) make it unlikely that the Jewish leaders would have arrested Jesus during Passover itself. This suggests that John's timing is more likely, though the timing of the Synoptic Gospels has, at least in some areas, more theological import.

This is especially true in Matthew, given its Jewish context. During the time of Jesus, Passover – as is clear in the Gospels – was a pilgrimage feast. This meant that three times a year (at Passover, Pentecost and Tabernacles), Jews were expected to journey to Jerusalem to celebrate the feast at the Temple. There is strong evidence that this did happen and that Jews from all over the diaspora did their best to travel to Jerusalem for the feast. The challenge came at the fall of the Temple. How would you celebrate the pilgrimage festivals without sacrifice? Rabbinic Judaism responded to this by instituting more fully a non-sacrificial domestic seder meal; Matthew's community (like Mark's and Luke's) responded by stressing the links between the Last Supper and Passover (See Matthew 26.17–20) and the importance of Jesus' death within this.

Judas

One of the key differences between Matthew's account of Jesus' death and those of the other Gospels is the importance of Judas within the narrative. This importance is achieved through Matthew's telling of Judas' death. Luke does give an account of Judas' death, in Acts 1.18–19, but it is included, it appears, largely to explain the need for a replacement disciple among the Twelve. It is also important to observe that in Acts Judas trips, falls and dies, whereas in Matthew it is his remorse at his actions that kills him. Indeed in Matthew, Judas is the foil to Peter. At the Last Supper Jesus says that both will betray him. Judas is identified as the one who will hand him over; Peter as the one who will deny him three times. Both Judas and Peter refuse to accept the designation – 'Surely not I, Rabbi?' (Matthew 26.25), and Peter's double refusal to believe that he will deny Jesus (Matthew 26.33–35) – and both go on to do exactly what Jesus said they would. The key difference between the two is that Judas succumbs to despair before Jesus has even died; whereas Peter, although despairing, continues. Indeed it is Matthew's Gospel that evokes the question of whether Judas' greatest sin was not so much betrayal as giving in to despair so that Jesus could not subsequently forgive him.

The crucifixion

The crucifixion of Jesus in Matthew largely follows Mark's account, with three main themes: Jesus is mocked, Jesus is given the title of 'King of the Jews', and Jesus' death is seen as a fulfilment of the Scriptures. Two key differences between Matthew's account and that in the other Gospels are, however, worth reflecting on briefly.

The first is a change in Jesus' reported quotation from Psalm 22.1: 'My God, my God, why have you forsaken me?' The change consists not in the translation of the verse but in the words quoted. Both Mark and Matthew cite the verse in Aramaic (which suggests that this is the language in which Jesus quoted the Scriptures), but whereas Mark has 'Eloi, Eloi', Matthew has 'Eli, Eli'. This has caused much discussion among scholars about whether, in Matthew, Jesus switched from Aramaic to Hebrew (since 'Eli, Eli' could be Hebrew in form), and if he did, what significance this might have. Many scholars today, however, would argue that both Eli and Eloi are legitimate Aramaic versions of the same word. The reason for the difference might be a very simple one: it may be there to explain why a bystander could think that Jesus was calling for Elijah when he was, in fact, quoting Scripture.

The irony of the misunderstanding is that readers of the Gospels know that one like Elijah – John the Baptist – has already recognized and acknowledged Jesus to be the Messiah, and that Elijah himself has already been present at Jesus' transfiguration. There is no need for Jesus to call on Elijah; his death on the cross is precisely that which marks him out to be who he is.

There has been much discussion among commentators about whether Jesus' cry from the cross is to be taken as a cry of desolation or a statement of hope. The issue is that Psalm 22 (which, Matthew implies, Jesus continues to cite; see 27.37) ends with statements of trust in God like 'All the ends of the earth shall remember and turn to the LORD' (22.27). In Matthew's Gospel, however, there is a good argument for seeing his cry from the cross as expressing the growing abandonment that Jesus has experienced from chapter 13 onwards. He has been rejected by his home town (13.53–58); then by the disciples (26.56); then by the crowds (27.15–26). It seems an obvious progression for Jesus to cry out against his final apparent abandonment by God. On the cross Jesus feels deeply alone, and the words of Psalm 22.1 express this more fully than any other words could.

The second key difference between Matthew's crucifixion account and the others are the signs and wonders that happen at Jesus' death. Although the veil in the Temple is torn in two elsewhere, Matthew emphasizes this by recording the way in which the earth itself was torn in two and the dead raised. The significance of this is that Matthew is making clear that, with Jesus' death, the world itself changed. The long-awaited intervention of God can now be seen to have begun (even if it hasn't finished). There are strong parallels between Matthew's account of the resurrection of the dead and Ezekiel 37.11–14, which speaks of the resurrection of the dry bones. In Ezekiel 37 the resurrection of the dry bones was a marker that the exile had come to an end; here Matthew uses similar imagery to argue that Jesus' death has now achieved that for which Israel has waited for so long. The exile is now at an end and God's people can be restored.

Imagining the text

Matthew's Gospel often presents its material in triads – a three-fold structure which some scholars have called a 'compositional habit' of the writer. This three-fold approach was common in ancient sources, and it may go back to the oral roots from which the written material was developed. It even seems possible that Jesus taught and spoke in threes. Matthew's narrative of the Passion is taken largely from Mark's Gospel, and in it we can see this same three-fold structure which gives great emphasis to the theological themes that the writer wants to stress in the story of Jesus' betrayal, trial, execution and burial. This poem uses a three-fold approach to meditate on the immensely powerful and theologically dense narrative of Jesus' final days.

Patterns in words . . .

In the garden,
three prayers of terror: 'Let this cup pass';
three prayers of trust: 'Your will be done';
three prayers unsaid: his followers asleep.

In the darkness,
three fearful treacheries: the kiss, the sword, the flight;
three pious priestly rants: the truth unheard;
three vehement denials: 'I do not know the man'.

In the morning,
three unjust conspiracies: Pilate, priests and people;
three handy props for mockery: the robe, the reed, the thorns;
three furious steps to murder: first isolate your victim, next
    scorn, then the kill.

In the daylight,
three filthy criminals: a cross for each;
three painful hours of agony: the nails, the nakedness, the
    thirst;
three tests of his obedience: to save himself, come down,
    defend his dignity.

In the end time,
three witnesses of death: the wakened saints, centurion, the
    women standing;
three powers to stifle life: the stone, the seal, the guards;
three faithful friends to wonder: rich Joseph, clearing up the
    mess; and Magdalene,
with the other Mary, both watching . . .

Reflecting on the text

Friendship

It is often easy to overlook the challenge that Jesus presents to us. The way he directs his prophecy to his listeners is by holding up a mirror to them, a mirror in which they can see the difference between the lives they are living and the promise of the kingdom of God. We might experience this both as judgement and as teaching.

Both prophecy and teaching were public events, delivered in the Temple, in front of the crowds, in full hearing of all. The scene to which we now turn our attention is of a very different kind. We see an intimate gathering of a dozen or so men and, probably, some women, who had mostly been together for at least a couple of years. They had shared much: adventure, adulation, hostility, danger. They had enthused each other, competed with each other, debated with each other, quarrelled with each other. They knew each other pretty well.

Early Christian art depicts Jesus wearing a philosopher's pallium and the disciples as enquiring students. Many of our hymns and prayers speak of him as king, Master, Lord, captain, and of his ancient and modern disciples as subjects, servants, soldiers. But if we believe what he did and what he said at that last supper he shared with Peter and the others, he is not a Master or Lord like any other, but himself a servant, and they are not servants (any more) but friends. Some of you may as children have been read to from a rather sentimental Ladybird children's book, *Jesus the Friend*: but the point being made here is not that he is our friend, but that we are, or may be, his friends. And, if his friends, then friends of God.

Friendship is one of the great human experiences. Christians, it has to be said, have however sometimes been suspicious of human friendships, seeing in them a potential obstacle in the relation of the self to God. Augustine, who seems to have had a more than usual gift for friendship, nevertheless reproached himself for the tears he wept at the death of a friend. These tears seemed to him to betray a lack of faith in God. Others have been more appreciative: the medieval writer Aelred of Rievaulx rewrote a line of St John's Gospel to read: 'he that abides in friendship abides in God, and God in him'.

But, whatever we might think of friendships with – well, our friends, it's not obvious that 'friendship' is a natural feature of our relation to God. Surely, the difference between God and human beings is too great for us to be friends. God is God and we are but as dust. How could there be friendship between two such unequal beings? Even to think of such a thing seems to betray that old familiar hubris of our wanting to be as gods, our wanting to claim a little bit of what is God's for ourselves. Perhaps that's why so few church buildings allow you to feel that going into God's house is like going to the house of a friend. This is not a home away from home. This is where you are taught to know your place!

Perhaps the worry is that, in the closeness of friendship, we will lose that sense of the majesty of God, the distance and ineffability of the Godhead that elicits our most sublime feelings of worship and adoration. Yet friendship does not mean that the friend is in every case simply another self, someone who likes the same clothes, enjoys the same music, has the same politics, practises the same religion as I do, although there are friendships like that. Many friends, like many marriages, are odd couples, as ill matched as chalk and cheese – and yet sometimes these are the best and strongest friendships.

Friends aren't, or don't have to be, the same in every respect. Friendship allows for difference, and sometimes, often, it's the very difference that makes the friendship so pleasurable. And of no one else is it as true as it is of our friends, that we rejoice in their joys, that we are glad for their successes, that we want them to have all the admiration and all the glory due them for their achievements. Their success is our success, even when what they have achieved is something we could never do and perhaps would never even want to do. 'I'm glad for you,' we say, and, when we mean it, that's as close as we get in human relationships to what worship is all about: giving what is God's to God: rejoicing in God and praising God for God's sake.

But perhaps there is also a worry that unless we insist on God's power over us and our duty of obedience to him, we'll never be sufficiently motivated really to change our lives for the better, really to start living like those who seek to give God what is God's. Being as we are, we humans need to have the whip cracked now and again. We need a God to respect, not a God to be chummy with. Yet this anxiety seems misplaced. After all, human experience shows that we are, on the whole, more likely to do more and to do it better for our friends than for our leaders, managers or teachers – perhaps even more than for our country. And the reason is obvious to anyone who has any experience of friendship. Because though friendships sometimes have to be worked at, and though friendship may sometimes seem too good to be believed, our friends' needs are as real to us as our own: as John Henry Newman said, 'Our first life is in ourselves, our second is in our friends': our friends are our other lives.

To know God in Christ as our friend is not to empty this relationship of challenge: it is rather to understand it in such a way that we become ever more motivated to do all, to give all, to suffer all when that's what is asked of us. And as the story of this last supper also reminds us, there is no betrayal so great, no pain of being betrayed so great, as when we are betrayed by a friend.

Lastly, to live with God as a friend is to live with God humbly. And perhaps this is really why the first and many subsequent disciples have been hesitant to see their Christian lives as friendship with God. James and John wanted to sit at Christ's right and at his left in his kingdom, to be his vice-regents. Paul hints that Peter fancied his role as the first of the apostles. Apostles, it seems, like the idea of sitting on thrones and judging Israel. Such pretensions have no place in friendship. Friendship with God means talking with him about the humble, everyday things you talk about with your friends: your life, your loves, your family, your clothes, your job, the weather. Far from encouraging us to think of ourselves 'as gods', thinking of ourselves as friends of God is the surest way to keep our Christian feet on the ground of humble, everyday reality.

Remembering the betrayal and last supper as we reflect on the text, we move from the public arena of the Temple to the intimacy of a private dinner, and from the public offices of prophecy and teaching to the intimacy of a circle of friends. And just as prophecy and teaching each holds up a mirror in which we are challenged to see ourselves, our hopes and our desires for what they really are, so too the company of friends, the circle of our other selves, focuses the image in that same mirror more sharply, because more intimately, and gives us to see – perhaps more clearly than we might like – what we really value, what, and who, really moves us. To claim God as our friend is not impiously to make ourselves 'as gods': it is to let God be as he wants to be, and to do for us what he wants to do for us, to be there for us in the way he wants to be, that seeing ourselves as we are in the mirror of his friendship we might wish to become more as he is, among us as servant – and as friend.

Action, conversation, questions, prayer

Action

Who are your friends, and is there challenge as well as security in your relationships? Is your congregation and community good at nurturing and making friendships?

Conversation and questions

- Pray to identify with Jesus in his suffering.
- What do you see in these last days of the life of Jesus?
- How was the mission of Jesus completed?
- To contemplate the story of Jesus is itself an act of thanksgiving.

Prayer

Lord, you break apart
Our communities,
Our securities,
Our images of you.
We thank for your abiding friendship,
Your fractured food in this Feast,
Where the human and divine meet,
Through Jesus, the heart of God.
Amen.

7

Easter

———————

Exploring the text

The stories of Jesus' resurrection begin, oddly perhaps to our minds, in the stories of his burial. The accounts of the burial of Jesus' body are often skipped over as we move from a focus on his death to his resurrection. However, all the Gospel accounts include a reference to Jesus' burial, and as we look at Matthew's account it becomes clear why these references are so important.

The burial and resurrection

The accounts of the burial of Jesus' body all point to a dispute between Christians and their opponents about the empty tomb. It is clear that everyone accepted that the tomb was empty; what was less accepted was *why* it was empty. Matthew's account carefully seeks to establish both that Jesus was really dead and that the location of his tomb was known to the chief priests and Pharisees. More than that, it argues that the body could not have been stolen by the disciples, because to have done so would have involved taking the body from under the noses of what we can presume were the Temple soldiers.

Matthew continued the theme of the Temple soldiers in the resurrection account, since Jesus' body was removed from the tomb under the noses of the soldiers – but not by the disciples, by resurrection. Another notable feature of Matthew is that it gets closer than any of the other Gospels to describing the moment of resurrection. In the other Gospels, Jesus was already raised, the stone rolled away and an angelic figure present by the time the women arrived at the tomb. Matthew appears to describe the moment itself; or at least the moment when the angel revealed the resurrection. As with the crucifixion, the moment of revelation is accompanied by an earthquake (as it was when the dead were raised at Jesus' death) and the Temple soldiers are rendered insensible with fear. The question that Matthew does not answer is whether this was the moment of resurrection itself. The angel's rolling away of the stone suggests that it might have been, but then why did the women not see Jesus leave the tomb? The other possibility is that Jesus has already been raised and has left the tomb without the stone having been rolled away.

The complexities raised by Matthew's account may explain the other unusual detail in the resurrection appearance. In Matthew, as in John, the women encounter the risen Jesus on the way back from the tomb. Then they come to him, take hold of his feet and worship him. The fact that they took hold of Jesus' feet could be taken simply as a description of their bodily position as they worshipped. The Greek word *proskuneo* has the resonance of prostration, and this is certainly the position from which it would be easiest to take hold of someone's feet. The question is, why make this explicit here? The answer is that this may be another subtle response to the criticisms of the Christian community's belief in Jesus' resurrection. The presence of the soldiers combated the suggestion that Jesus' body had been stolen, and the taking hold of his feet might have combated a suggestion that what they saw was a ghost. In the Greco-Roman worldview, ghosts had no feet. Therefore the fact that the women took hold of Jesus' feet to worship him argued strongly that he was no ghost. This might have been all the more necessary given Matthew's own account, which does not appear to explain how the risen Jesus left the tomb.

Worshipping, doubting and being sent

The women were not the only ones to worship the risen Jesus. When the disciples met him on the mountain in Galilee, Matthew tells us that they worshipped but that something else happened as well. There has been extensive grammatical discussion in scholarship about precisely who doubted. The little construction *hoi de* (which prefaces the verb doubt) can in some instances suggest a change of subject. The problem is that Matthew does not make it clear who the change of subject refers to. As a result the phrase can either mean 'they worshipped but some doubted' or 'they worshipped and they doubted'. In a sense there is little effective difference between the two. Whether some or all of the disciples were present, worship and doubt existed at the same time during their encounter with the risen Jesus.

This causes some commentators concern, and it is worth pausing to reflect on it. The problem may lie with our modern use of the word doubt, which is often used as a synonym for unbelief. We must be very clear that the opposite of believing is unbelieving. Matthew does not state that the disciples did not believe, but that they doubted. This verb is used elsewhere in Matthew with Peter's ill-fated attempt to walk to Jesus on the water from the boat. He sank, Matthew tells us, because he doubted (Matthew 14.31). The point is that he never doubted that it was Jesus, nor that he wanted to get to Jesus; he doubted because of the storm. The Greek verb (*distazō*) suggests that doubting involves holding more than one thing in your mind at any one time. The disciples, then, encountered the risen Jesus but, like Peter on the water, held in their minds other concerns at the same time. Indeed one could argue that doubting is a very good place to begin worship, because it is when we truly lose the capacity to think out everything to our own satisfaction that we are most likely to be able to encounter who God really is.

It is also worth noting that, immediately following on from the doubting, Jesus commissioned the disciples to make other disciples, baptizing and teaching them in the name of the Father and of the Son and of the Holy Spirit. Clearly Jesus did not feel the need to wait until their doubt had dissipated before committing to them the most important task of all: the proclamation of the kingdom. This is a striking difference from our modern way of acting. So often today we feel the need to wait until we are absolutely confident that we understand everything, are well trained and primed to go. Then, and only then, are we prepared to set out and proclaim the good news of Jesus Christ, Son of God who died and rose again. It appears that Jesus had no similar sensitivities. In verse 19, he sent the disciples who, just two verses before, had been doubting as they worshipped. Jesus, it seems, does not need us to be ready, he just needs us to go.

Imagining the text

The Gospel reading for Easter Day (Matthew 28.1–10) tells the story of the two women who go to the tomb early in the morning – Mary Magdalene and 'the other Mary'. They want to 'see the tomb' – to witness the place of Jesus' burial in the same way as they have witnessed his life – for these women, along with others, have followed Jesus from Galilee as his disciples, and have funded his ministry; they witnessed his crucifixion (27.55–56), and they saw the dead body of Jesus being deposited in the tomb, which was closed over by a great stone (27.57–61). Matthew tells how this tomb was then sealed and guarded (27.62–66). When the two Marys reach the tomb they encounter a terrifying, dazzling angel who rolls away the stone and reveals to them the astonishing news of the resurrection, inviting them to look into the empty tomb as pilgrims might do: these women are witnesses to the resurrection. The angel then commands them to take the news to the other disciples – that Jesus has gone ahead of them and is inviting them to return to Galilee and meet him there. As they run to do this missionary work they encounter Jesus himself, and he gives them the same greeting, 'Do not be afraid', and the same commission: 'go and tell my brothers that they will see me in Galilee'. Matthew describes the Galilee encounter and the commission Jesus gives there to the 11 (male) disciples in the last verses of the Gospel (28.16–19).

This poem imagines the two women called Mary addressing the male disciples. It speaks of the women's power and joy as they tell their brothers in faith the story of their experience of the dazzling light of the angel, of being witnesses to the empty tomb. They explain their conviction that Jesus is going before them, and relate their encounter with the risen Christ, and the power of his commission to them to be the witnesses of his resurrection just as they have been witnesses to his ministry, execution and burial. The resurrection is an unsealing not only of the tomb, but of women's power to speak, inspire and guide others towards the mystery of the risen Christ at work among them and before them, sending the Church out into the world and fulfilling the ancient hopes of Israel to be the source of God's salvation to the nations of the world. The emphasis on journey and place, on seeing and witnessing key events and specific locations in the life, death and resurrection of Jesus, which Matthew gives to the women's experience, seems to suggest a theme of pilgrimage too: a spiritual gravity which will pull pilgrims to Jerusalem as the place in which the Saviour dies and rises, even as the power of that death and resurrection sends out his followers throughout the world to make new disciples and baptize into the life of Father, Son and Holy Spirit.

The unsealing

Having followed him, and watched, and listened to the teaching,
to the death cries and his final breath,
we asked 'How many years have we made journeys from our homes
for this?'
Day after day we shared our wine, our bread, our oil, our tears;
we never closed our purses to his needs, nor yours.

Surprised pilgrims, that same urge to witness
led us walking to the grave
that sudden morning when
our bitter hours of grief untwisted into tongues for telling
the unfathomable powers of
meeting with the one who was complete
yet more.

To us his presence had the quality of dawn,
light's blaze, a body welcomed into spirit,
himself beyond himself,
a place reached and superseded all at once,
not destination, but for us the thrill of being found
by him whom we have looked for, looked for, looked for.

Listen brothers, this is what we women come to share.
Now is the season of unsealing,
the final, endless breaking open,
the pouring out of water and of truth.
Now we have gifts to give: blood energy
in which the past shall fuel us for a time of travelling
and making whole:
from Galilee a time of going out;
for Jerusalem a time of bringing in;
a time of living through the end
with joy.

Reflecting on the text

Matthew 28.1–10: The women discover the tomb empty and report their findings – with joy and fear, both fitting reactions to the wonder of the day.

Many years ago as a student I attended the funeral of a much-loved parish priest. He was faithful, amusing, certainly eccentric, but with a heart as deep as any well. At all times of the day and night, he could be seen cycling around his parish in a black cassock, sometimes smoking – quite a sight, as you might imagine! The sight was more amusing because, fearing baldness, this holy man had grown a length of hair on the right side of his head above his ear, and carefully arranged it to cover his bald head. He collapsed and died of a heart attack while cycling back from a baptism visit on a local housing estate.

His funeral was a splendid occasion. It was a pontifical celebration, with the Bishop trying to outdo the Pope! The parish priest had once warned me that one should be aware of men in funny hats . . . The church was packed with flocks of servers, a flood of acolytes, herds of assistant priests and a little galaxy of bishops. However, what struck me most was the number of ordinary people from across the community, many of whom did not usually darken the doors of the church, but now came to pay their respects. It was clear that I was not the only person who had respect and affection for this priest, as I looked around and saw many who wept for their much-loved vicar.

The Bishop addressed the congregation with these words:

'Dear friends, we are an Easter people – the followers of the risen Christ should not grieve – this is not the time for tears but joy.' This command, this affirmation of faith, had little effect upon the congregation, who continued to express their feelings as they wept.

I have often wondered what it means to be an Easter people. As we read again these verses from Matthew 28, what does it mean – in our individualistic, materialistic, distracted and busy world – to have a faith? What difference does faith mean to us, especially in our experience of sadness, fear and pain? Any seasoned observer of human nature will know that it is hard to shift and change people's lives. We live in a world which is beautiful but also scarred and disfigured by human sin and weakness.

Matthews's narrative of Easter speaks into our experience of life where little is certain, fixed or secure. Sometimes, like that congregation all those years ago, our bodies are overcome with a sense of the sheer fragility of life, and the tears emerge despite our best efforts.

Faith must deal with what lies in our hearts and minds, and we as Christian disciples must be honest about our resentments, our grief, our hatreds and suspicions. Complacency and self-interest still dominate on the horizons of our life.

So what is faith in an Easter God? We are reminded in Matthew's account of the resurrection that there is both fear and joy in such faith. It is not a protection from the difficulties and challenges that face us in life. Being an Easter people does not mean that any of us will not require a handkerchief to mop up our tears; all of us know deep in our hearts what our lives are like and how much has been struggle. As human beings we have to deal with our fears and the reality of how little control we are able to exercise over circumstances and experiences. It is into this condition of who and where we are that God touches us with Easter life and hope. Easter peace is not the obliteration of our past or present, but the redrawing of our lives into a new way of seeing. Faith gives us the opportunity for direction, redirection, meaning and depth in the lives, ordinary and sometimes complex as they are, that we struggle to live for the good.

As we see in the experience of the early visitors to the tomb, we should never underestimate the power of God to transform and change and make new. What may seem to be beyond our heart or understanding is not beyond the healing and transformative power and love of God. However partial or limited our faith may be, there are no limits on salvation. The self-offering of Jesus on the cross is healing for every place, every experience, every person and every community, a peace for every injury, pain and prejudice. The tree of the cross must take root in these dead places of heart and mind and so enable Easter to be truly a rising. The transforming grace of God bears fruit in us by the Holy Spirit, who turns us continually Godward, continually outwards to our neighbour in love.

We can be confident but we must safeguard against triumphalism, which does not listen carefully to human experience and its sensitivities. We can nurture faith that embraces doubt, that grows through honesty and openness. There is in the telling of the resurrection story a kind of grief, a sort of dim sorrowing light, seeing through tears, as if the dawning truth of freedom and release and resurrection spills out of the bewilderment and anguish and searching.

Jesus comes to us, as he did to those early women at the tomb, as we are and where we are. That is the message in the resurrection story for us all. Jesus greets the lonely, offers presence with the grieving, peace to those who are fearful, an invitation to the doubting, and direction for the futile. This is a call to all who can find his hope and follow him in love. This is resurrection in our hearts and minds, in and through our fears, among the dead, in our cities and on our journey.

Action, conversation, questions, prayer

Action

Reread the Easter narratives from Matthew – and reflect on the joy and fear present in them. What are your fears and joys as you celebrate the victory of Easter?

Conversation and questions

- We pray not to forget the revolution that being a Christian must mean for us.

- What are the events and experiences that clinch Christian faith for us?
- Pray for the gift of pure trust, the true sign of love – not demanding proofs or measurable recompense.

Prayer

God of new creation,
From the womb of the earth
You raised the Lord of life:
May we receive the word of women
And meet him in the dawning light;
May we live with morning joy
That love will never die,
Through Jesus Christ, the resurrection and the life.
Amen.

8

Ordinary Time

━━━━━◆◦◆◦◆━━━━━

Exploring the text

One of the themes of Matthew's Gospel that recurs over and over again (and especially in the readings that appear during Ordinary Time) is the theme of what it means to be a community, and in particular what it means to be the Jesus community.

The *ekklesia* and the Matthean community

A fact that many people know about Matthew's Gospel is that Matthew is the only Gospel writer to use the Greek word *ekklesia*, which is often translated as 'church'. He uses the word twice: once in 16.18 and then again more extensively in 18.15–22. It is often assumed by scholars that this usage of the word is symptomatic of Matthew's particular concern for the welfare of his own community (for more on this see the Introduction, p. 12).

It is certainly interesting to notice that this word has a particular potential resonance for a Jewish-focused community. When people talk about the early Church's use of the word *ekklesia* as a descriptor of their own community, mention is often made of Greek city states where the word *ekklesia* was used to describe full citizens of the city who had voting rights within it. In that context, the use by early Christians of the word *ekklesia* suggests that it is making some kind of statement about the Christians having their citizenship elsewhere. But in a Jewish context the word has a different resonance. In the Septuagint the Hebrew word *qahal* or assembly, the word used to describe the gathering of God's people, was usually translated as *sunagoge* (from which comes our English word synagogue) but occasionally as *ekklesia*. In a Jewish context, the usage of the word *ekklesia* allowed the community to identify themselves with a theological word which meant God's gathered people without using the word – synagogue – that was already in widespread use by their enemies. The word *ekklesia*, then, allowed Matthew's community to define themselves over and against their Jewish rivals.

However, in chapter 18 Matthew presents some powerful arguments about behaviour within the *ekklesia*. Matthew 18.15–22 addresses the attitude both of an individual who sins and of the rest of the community to that individual. In terms of the individual, it is interesting to observe that the Matthean community followed the same three-step procedure as the Essene community at Qumran (see *The Community Rule*, 1QS 5.24—6.1). There, as in Matthew 18, the individual should first be made aware privately of the sin that has been committed. Then, if no action is taken, the reproof should be made public within the community; only then, if the person takes no notice, should he be expelled from the community. It is impossible to know whether the overlap between the Matthean community 'rule' and that of the Essenes at Qumran reflects a general attitude to the way in which communities worked in first-century Judaism, or whether there was a more specific historical overlap between the two communities.

If the community's response to the sin of an individual appears harsh, it is worth remembering two important facts about this command. The first is that it is to be enacted with Matthew 18.21–22 in mind. In other words, no limit is to be placed on the forgiveness which the community must offer to anyone who sins. The point is not whether a person sins but whether he repents. If the person does repent, then it is incumbent upon the community to forgive that person times without number. The Greek word in verse 22 could be translated as either 77 or seven times seventy (i.e. 490 times), but the precise number involved is less important than the fact that it refers back to Genesis 4.24: 'If Cain is avenged sevenfold, truly Lamech seventy-sevenfold'. In other words, Lamech promised revenge without limit in Genesis; the Matthean community is to respond with forgiveness in a similar manner.

The second point to bear in mind is that the expelled community member is to become like a Gentile or a tax collector. The pairing of these two has particular significance in Matthew if we remember both that the disciples are sent to the 'nations' (i.e. the Gentiles) in Matthew 28.19 and the tradition that the author of the Gospel was a tax collector. What Matthew 18.17 means, then, is that the expelled member of the church was to be treated as you would *any* Gentile or tax collector: that is as someone for whom the kingdom is designed. Expulsion from the community should not result in the cold shoulder but in special care for the person's welfare and return to the kingdom.

The harvest is plentiful

The other feature to bear in mind about the community in Matthew's Gospel is that it is an outward-facing community. This is emphasized not only in Matthew 28.16–20 but in numerous other places throughout the Gospel as well. One of those places is Matthew 9.35—10.4, which acts as a bridge between Jesus' deeds of power in Matthew 8—9 and his sending of the Twelve in chapter 10. In 9.35—10.4, Matthew makes it clear that Jesus both integrated the disciples into his ministry of teaching, proclaiming and healing and then sent them outwards to join him in proclaiming the kingdom.

The large blocks of teaching that we find in Matthew remind us how important it was for Jesus to teach his disciples while he was with them. But this is coupled, as it is in the other Gospels, with a clear intention that the teaching should be passed on, that the proclamation of the kingdom should not stay just with those that Jesus met but should be passed on by his disciples. It is worth noticing, however, that in Matthew's Gospel they are sent initially to proclaim the kingdom only to the lost sheep of Israel. Matthew's is a two-stage proclamation: first to Israel and then to the 'nations'. And the community is the place where this proclamation must take place.

Imagining the text

In Year A, the first Sunday of Ordinary Time begins with Jesus teaching his disciples that faith is more than claims and spoken promises – it is a matter of changed hearts which find expression in concrete behaviour (Matthew 7.21–29, Proper 4). The following Sunday tells the story of Jesus calling Matthew to leave his lucrative and exploitative life as a tax collector, and to follow him in a radically different way of life. This story of the call of Matthew shows how Jesus made friends of people who were excluded and regarded as sinful. Jesus' ministry is characterized by compassion and healing (9.9–13, 18–26, Proper 5). These practical values of reconciliation and inclusion are a mark of the kingdom of God, which he embodies through the ways in which he lives out his relationships with others. Those who follow Jesus are to live according to the same kingdom values, which will not be understood or appreciated by those who do not hear the good news of the kingdom. His followers will attract hostility and encounter suffering because they have a different way of seeing how God is at work in the world, but they find their satisfaction and fulfilment in God's grace, in Jesus their inspiration and strengthener (Proper 6, 7, 8 and 9).

For a person such as Matthew, called to a new way of living as he follows Jesus, there will be a new way of seeing the world and a different way of relating to others, a way which is

89

kingdom-shaped. In the spiritual economy of which he is now part, as a redeemed sinner depending very consciously on the grace of God whom he has encountered in Jesus, he learns new ways of thinking and behaving; he values different things from those he once prized: for him there is a new way of counting. The same is true for every disciple, individually and also for the whole community of believers who now make up the church.

From his boat on the lake Jesus teaches his followers to see with kingdom eyes and to be expectant of good things which can be appreciated by kingdom-shaped hearts (Proper 10). This poem celebrates the new ways of appreciating God's action taught and enacted by Jesus. God's generosity of grace cannot be squandered even by failure, resistance or doubt, even among those who are his disciples (Proper 10, 11, 14, 17, 23).

Kingdom ways of counting

When examining disciples,
how does the teacher
mark success?
Take as the measure
not right answers, but the life that is lived.

When testing the medicine,
how does the doctor
know who's healed?
Look deep into eyes, to find
compassion for the sick.

When hearing the beloved talk,
how does the lover
sound out truth?
Listen for night whispers called
in cold light of day.

When estimating harvest,
how does the farmer
gauge the yield?
Plan for weeds and wilting barren parts,
then sow generously the whole field.

When guiding hungry people,
how does the leader
feed the crowds?
Bless what they have to give,
make their little God's enough.

Reflecting on the text

The good life in community?

What is your philosophy? By what values do you live? Does all this church make a difference?

Perhaps in Europe we have come to live by Descartes' oft-quoted aphorism: 'I think, therefore I am'. In Africa, in contrast, being human is expressed as I belong, therefore I am. I remember meeting a refugee at a meeting in Birmingham about asylum seekers. This woman had escaped from Iraq; she said, 'Now I can die in England because I know there will be people at my funeral.' She belonged. And the Church had enabled that belonging. It had given her a home. Desmond Tutu translates the African concept of *ubuntu* as 'a person is a person through a person'. Let me put it like this. When someone asks, 'Are you well?', the response is, 'I am well if you are well.'

This sense of belonging is a fundamental spiritual need. It is what we try to nurture in our communities and churches. A place of welcome where all belong.

We are social animals. Throughout human history life has been lived in the context of communities of one sort or another. But communities can be good and bad. They can include and exclude. They have ups and downs. We don't always behave ourselves!

The bad is easy to recognize, because the history of humankind is as much as anything a history of war and conflict. We read in the record of the past and see in the news of our day that humans have great difficulty getting along with one another – whether it be in the neighbourhood, village, city, state, nation or world.

As Christians we understand the negative side of community life, and we confess it. Furthermore, our faith and commitment presses us to develop the best side of our lives as social creatures.

The primary prayer of Christian faith begins OUR – not 'my' but 'our'. It is a shared prayer for a shared faith. We understand ourselves as part of a family in which we are all brothers and sisters. We recognize that our lives in the context of community must be mutually supportive.

Jesus says, 'Where two or three are gathered in my name, I am there among them.' If any group of us will gather, work, act with the Holy Spirit guiding us, with God's spirit intentionally a part of what we do, we become much more than simply the collective number of people we are. Two becomes more than two, and three becomes more than three. The sum of our individual ideas and resources and abilities becomes much more because of the synergy that God's presence provides.

We do gather in Jesus' name. We re-call him to presence with us. And that makes him a part of us and of what we do. That is what we experience at each Eucharist – we in him and he in us. But we don't celebrate the Eucharist alone. If no one but the priest shows up for a midweek service, for instance, there will be no celebration of the Eucharist. There is no community for whom to break bread.

Ours is a faith of community – of twos and threes and fours – but never of individuals. We act together so we can help one another and so we can work in God's name, thereby multiplying our resources and ability to do what God calls us to do. Our community is the lifeline to the experience of God and to the power of God moving among God's people.

While a private spiritual and prayer life is essential for each of us, it is likely to become dry and turn inward if it is not infused with regular doses of shared worship and connection with others, gathered in Christ's name, and for his sake. 'Where two or three are gathered in my name, I am there among them.' The gathering – the connectedness – magnifies the Spirit for us and in us and with us.

Jesus makes it clear how important we are one to another. Through our link to one another through Christ, there is a power and possibility in our community. There is much more work to do in building and developing this community. There are many more welcomes to be extended. We must safeguard against complacency and self-satisfaction. We must work together to make life-giving love more effective among God's people in this place. We come together, we stay together, we work together in all the tensions, the ups and downs for growth and transformation.

Ubuntu. I am well if you are well.

Action, conversation, questions, prayer

Action

Think about one small act that will build up your community.

Conversation and questions

- How do we welcome people into our community?
- Praise God for those who care about and for you.
- What part do you play in making the gospel known?
- How do we learn to trust in the provision of God?
- Is habit a strength or blockage for true religion? Or is it both?

Prayer

Trinity of love,
Deposing the powers
Of hate and isolation;
Gathering creation
In bonds of mutual care:
Through the waters of baptism
May our relationships be reborn
In justice, mercy and peace:
Through Jesus Christ, who is with us always.
Amen.

9

The Sundays before Advent

Exploring the text

During the Sundays leading up to Advent the Lectionary draws our attention to the theme of watching and waiting. It is slightly odd that, although on the fourth Sunday before Advent we have the opening verses of Matthew 24, we do not have 24.15–51. The problem with this is that the second half of Matthew 24 sets the themes for the three parables that follow in chapter 25. Verses 1–14 of chapter 24 focus more on the events that will accompany the end, whereas in 15–51 we turn our attention to the attitude that must be adopted while waiting for the end. The parables in chapter 25 (the wise and foolish virgins, the talents, and the sheep and the goats) all emphasize overlapping yet slightly different characteristics about the manner in which we wait for the end.

Matthew's parables

Matthew has two major blocks of parables: those in chapter 13 and the ones here in chapter 25. As a result, although Matthew's Gospel has fewer parables than Luke's, they become highly significant in Matthew because they form the content of two discourses (the third and the fifth). The parables, then, become in Matthew one of Jesus' primary methods of teaching.

Another feature to notice is that the parables in Matthew are all introduced as being ways to understand the kingdom of heaven: 'the kingdom of heaven is like . . .' One issue that modern readers often overlook is that the parables are meant to come

95

to us as something of a surprise. The kingdom of heaven is like yeast? Are you sure? The problem we have these days is that we are so used to the kingdom being compared to yeast, mustard seeds, pearls, etc., that we no longer take the time to wrestle with the image and attempt to work out in what way the kingdom of heaven could possibly resemble such unlikely things.

Even more intriguingly, chapter 25 opens with a statement of what the kingdom of heaven *will* be like. The construction is also used in Matthew 7.24 and 26: 'Everyone then who hears these words of mine and acts on them will be like a wise man who built his house on rock . . .' The difference seems to be that the parables in Matthew 13 state what the kingdom of heaven has already become and so Jesus' followers must explore the ways in which they can see these characteristics of the kingdom now. The construction used in 25.1 refers to what the kingdom will become and the markers that need to be looked for then. This point is emphasized by the content of the parables, which focus attention on a climactic moment in the future (whether it is the arrival of the bridegroom, the return of the king, or the judgement of the sheep and the goats).

What becomes clear from this construction is that now the kingdom of heaven grows swiftly and secretly and like treasure beyond price; then the kingdom will be like times when judgement takes place. The kingdom of heaven is not a place of judgement now, but it will become such a place in the future.

The nature of the judgement

In chapter 25 Matthew goes on to explore the grounds upon which judgement will be made. The parables follow on one from another. The first, the parable of the bridesmaids, seems to be focused almost entirely on the theme of readiness. The wise bridesmaids are those who are in a state of constant readiness for the bridegroom; the foolish ones those who leave practical arrangements for later. In the context in which we find the parable in the Gospel it seems most likely that underlying it is a critique of those who do not take the coming of the Son of Man seriously. Within first-century Judaism there were Jews who believed very strongly that God's climactic intervention into the world was imminent; others who believed it was not. It is very likely that a similar disagreement existed within the Jewish Christian community between those who believed that the Son of Man would come very soon and those who did not (indeed some scholars believe that the Gospel of Luke is an early example of a writing that downplayed the imminence of the coming of the Son of Man).

The next parable, the parable of the talents, is slightly different. The focus here is not on readiness for the arrival of the Son of Man, but the effectiveness with which one has worked before the return of the master. The attitude of the master towards the servant who hid his 'talents' in the ground seems exceedingly harsh until you place this parable alongside the parable of the hidden treasure in Matthew 13.44. In the days before banking, hiding treasure in the ground was a popular means of safeguarding your goods. As this parable illustrates, however, it was a risky business (especially if the field did not belong to you), as you were in constant danger of someone buying the field and stealing your treasure. Given that in Matthew the major command of Jesus to his disciples was to proclaim the gospel, the impact of this parable seems to be the question of how well the disciples work with the treasure (the teachings of Jesus) left to them.

The final parable in this series – that of the sheep and the goats – is often interpreted on its own. As is often the case, however, doing so diminishes the impact of the context in which it is found. If the parable of the talents raises the question of how effectively the disciples of Jesus work with the teachings of Jesus, the parable of the sheep and the goats may well be focused on the question of how the different nations of the world responded to the proclamation of the gospel. Although this parable is often interpreted as a call to each Christian to care for the poor and imprisoned, its internal logic suggests that this may not be the right interpretation. The problem is that when judgement happens it is of 'the nations'. Although this possibly refers to individuals within the nations, a plainer reading would be that each nation is judged on the way in which it responds to 'the least of these', a phrase which elsewhere in Matthew refers to Christians.

If this interpretation is accepted, the message of the parables grows as we move through the chapter: all should act in constant readiness for the return of the Son of Man. This involves working carefully with the treasure of the gospel left to us, because judgement will be made on the grounds of the way in which the nations have responded to the bearers of this message when the Son does return. In addition, those not ready, and those who have not worked carefully with the treasure, will also find themselves locked out of the kingdom.

In many ways it seems appropriate to end a year exploring Matthew's Gospel with these difficult texts. As we observed in the Introduction, Matthew's harsh tone and his inclusion of judgement often make the Gospel difficult for us to receive. Much of our exploration of Matthew has been of parts of the Gospel which include fewer of these judgemental themes, but it would be wrong to end without drawing them back into our consideration. What becomes clear if you read Matthew 24—25 as a whole is that the Gospel was written at a time when fear and conflict were rife. It is at times like this that you most need a message that offers encouragement to keep going even when the pressure seems unbearable. Matthew 24—25 encourages its readers to recognize the severity of what is happening around them, but at the same time to keep their eyes firmly fixed on the horizon.

The challenge that these passages offer to us is how to handle them at a time that is less pressured and when the expectation of 'the end' has significantly diminished, if not disappeared altogether.

Imagining the text

The Gospel readings for the Sundays before Advent begin with a picture of Jesus sitting on the Mount of Olives looking down towards the city of Jerusalem, where his disciples have marvelled at the extraordinary temple constructed by Herod as a symbol of his piety and power (24.1–14). Jesus teaches them not to put their ultimate trust in human structures – material, religious or ideological. They are not to be distracted by the pain of persecution or the turmoil of crisis events, but to live their lives looking for the kingdom of God, in accordance with its demands, in the light of which they will be judged. The parables that follow in succeeding weeks – of the wise and foolish brides-maids (25.1–13), of the talents (25.14–30), and of the sheep and goats (25.31–46) – evoke for faithful disciples the absolute necessity to be alert and attentive to the values of God's kingdom and to the character of divine judgement that flows from them.

Living in the last days

What are you expecting
as the king comes near?
A gift like Herod's stones
beautiful and vast?
A majestic structure?
Temples golden in the sun?
Do not hope too much for these:
all broken down, every one.

What signal are you watching
as the child comes near?
  The gestures of a leader
  claims persuasive and strong?
  News of wrangles, wars and famines?
  Indications of collapse?
All these cries scream 'Crisis!'
None is the birth.

What sorrows are you nursing
as the healer comes near?
  The hurt of persecutions
  of hatreds undeserved?
  The cuts of betrayal?
  The burns of love grown cold?
Each injury is wounding
but not the end.

What guest are you expecting
as the traveller comes near?
  An absent lord returning?
  The delayed groom arriving?
  An investor now demanding?
  A hidden saviour begging?
Keep longing, looking, loving, giving
until he brings the completing.

Reflecting on the text

Matthew 25.31–46

The separation of the sheep from the goats appears only in
this Gospel, and so its imagery and disturbing implications
might ask us to attend to the text. The parable is colourful

in its description of justice and judgement. It is part of a long section of Matthew's narrative relating to the latter days of Jesus' life and ministry. This is important because we should remember that by this time the ministry of Jesus is in significant difficulty. He has predicted the fall of Jerusalem and the destruction of the Temple. His thoughts and messages have obviously turned towards the end of his work and thus the focus becomes the ultimate confrontation between God and the people.

It is difficult to stay with these words, not least because we Christians have been prematurely rather good at enforcing the divisions between the sheep and goats in the here and now. The picture of judgement portrayed here is impossible to square with human experience, in part because the basic simile is flawed. The separation of sheep and goats is a separation of animals of different kinds, a separation made not on the basis of what the animals have done, but based upon their inherent differences one from another. To comprehend the judgement of God via this image is to posit a determination that leads ultimately to either predestination or hopelessness. In this respect we should never forget the difficulties that lie in reading, imagining and interpreting the text. It demands from us time and courage and patience.

There is further difficulty with the text, in that it might encourage us to assume that certain works lead to righteousness and that apathy leads to damnation. On the face of it, that is probably not a bad assumption. But it does seem to contradict other texts, like the parable of the workers who come late to the field and walk away with compensation equal to those who have toiled all day, and the parable of the prodigal son, in whose story the abundance of grace is presented. To make a causal relationship between good deeds and salvation is to encourage a task-based righteousness, to suggest that the relationship with God is always predicated upon our behaviour.

So what are we to make of this text? Consider this – no one in this story knew their standing with God. Those who had been gracious, even extravagant, in the exercise of love had no idea that the consequences of their actions would be rewarded with God's benefactions. Those who had merely gone about their own business, being neither particularly nasty nor enthusiastic in their dealings with others, had no notion that the consequences of either their actions or their apathy would be the wrath of eternal damnation. It could be that the central point of this story is that we never know!

So it is our presumption of divine knowledge that is our presenting sin – not only the presumption that we can determine our own status, but also that we can discern the state of others. This is made obvious in the story. For in the end, it is not what the people actually do that distinguishes them. It is not their deeds, but their fundamental attitude towards one another that betrays them. The significant difference between the blessed and the damned in this story is that the blessed presumed everyone in need and saw everyone as related to themselves, while the damned presumed no need at all and saw no connection between their lives and the lives of others.

The blessed have extended themselves to everyone, the damned to no one. The charity administered by the blessed is given without presumption, without distinction. How else could they have been so unfailingly generous? Not every hunger is of the stomach, not every thirst is evident in a parched mouth, not every alienation is geographic or tribal, not every vulnerability is manifest in nakedness, not every sickness hospitalizes, not every imprisonment is behind bars. They have engaged every individual encountered, and to everyone they have extended themselves.

It is the charity that is withheld that condemns those captives. It was withheld without thinking. They say they saw no hunger even in the emaciated, no thirst even in the faint, no alienation even in the sojourner, no vulnerability even in those stripped of clothes, no sickness even in the broken, no imprisonment even among the shackled. They probably no longer even saw the other person. And when they did, they presumed – as many of us do – that whatever the state of the other, it was a state wilfully chosen and well deserved.

What this division of the end times encourages is not that we should suddenly embrace good deeds in the hope of reward or the fear of punishment. It is rather that we should move beyond our presumptions of each other and of God's judgement. We are to abandon what we do not know and cannot know in favour of what we do know and can know. If we are honest, we do know that we are not self-sufficient, nor are our lives unrelated. If we are faithful and believing, we can know the gift of eternal life in one another. Beyond that, you never know.

Action, conversation, questions, prayer

Action

Consider ways in which you might be stirred into vigilance before God.

Conversation and questions

- Consider the ways that God prods us in the direction of what we both need and deserve.
- May we love God even when he threatens?
- Christ rules by love: can we accept such kingship?
- How do you experience God as Maker and redeemer?

Prayer

Merciful Lord,
You resist all control and manipulation,
You are one with the hungry,
The naked and the scorned:
May our faith not be proved in dogma and piety,
But in serving you in one another,
In the last and the least,
Through Jesus Christ, our Saviour.
Amen.

Further reading and resources

There are many good commentaries on Matthew's Gospel. The one you choose will be down to your own personal taste. The list below is not exhaustive but gives you a sense of some of the most important works.

Lighter commentaries

Wright, Tom, *Matthew for Everyone* (2 vols), 2nd edn (London: SPCK, 2004).
   Tom Wright's excellent series, The Bible for Everyone, combines clear exegesis with an easy-to-read style.
Luz, Ulrich, *The Theology of the Gospel of Matthew* (Cambridge: Cambridge University Press, 1995).
   This is not a commentary but an introduction to the major themes of Matthew, and as such is very useful.
Jones, Ivor H, *The Gospel of Matthew* (London: Epworth Press, 1994).
   This short commentary is written for preachers and so would be a useful start for those beginning to preach on the Gospel.
Riches, John, *Matthew* (London: T & T Clark, 2004).
   This brief commentary in the T & T Clark Study Guide series is an excellent distillation of scholarship on Matthew's Gospel.

Larger commentaries

France, R. T., *The Gospel of Matthew*, New International Commentary on the New Testament (Grand Rapids: William B. Eerdmans, 2007).
Nolland, John, *The Gospel of Matthew*, New International Greek Testament Commentary (Grand Rapids: William B. Eerdmans, 2005).
   Both France's and Nolland's commentaries feature careful, thoughtful engagement with the text. Each represents the fruits of years of careful, faithful exploration of Matthew's Gospel, though they are often quite technical.

Davies, Margaret, *Matthew – Readings: A New Biblical Commentary*, 2nd edn (Sheffield: Sheffield Phoenix Press, 2009).

A particular strength of this commentary is the way it offers interpretations of particular events and strands of teaching by linking them with the bigger literary themes of Matthew's Gospel, helping the reader to appreciate the impact Matthew might have intended for early Christian audiences as well as the significance for contemporary times.

Keener, C., *Gospel of Matthew: A Socio-Rhetorical Commentary* (Grand Rapids: William B. Eerdmans, 2009).

Keener's commentary pays close attention to the world of Matthew and to the ways in which the Gospel communicates its message. Much less detailed and technical than Nolland and France, it brings the world of the gospel to life.

Minear, Paul S., *Matthew: The Teacher's Gospel* (Eugene, OR: Wipf & Stock, 2003).

This unusual but very helpful commentary concentrates on the Gospel's role in teaching. It looks constantly for connections between the way in which Matthew educates its audience and the way in which we attempt to teach today. Its unusual perspective makes it a helpful volume to include alongside other commentaries on Matthew.

Luz, Ulrich. *Matthew: A Commentary*, (3 vols), ed. Helmut Koester (Minneapolis: Augsburg Fortress, 2007).

No list of commentaries on Matthew would be complete without a mention of Luz's three-volume work. It is the Rolls-Royce of Matthew commentaries – detailed, scholarly, technical and very expensive. It won't be for most readers, but if you become serious about your study of Matthew you can do no better than this.

Some other useful books

Luz, Ulrich, *Studies in Matthew* (Grand Rapids: William B Eerdmans, 2005).

As will have become clear from the comments above, Luz is one of the most respected commentators on Matthew. His collection of articles on the Gospel will provide a good sense of the major issues in its study.

Saldarini, Anthony J., *Matthew's Christian-Jewish Community*, 2nd edn (Chicago: University of Chicago Press, 1994).

Stanton, Graham N., *Gospel for a New People: Studies in Matthew* (Louisville: Westminster/John Knox Press, 2004).

One of the key questions for the study of Matthew's Gospel is what, if anything, we can discover about Matthew's community. Both Saldarini and Stanton address this issue well.

James Woodward is a Canon of Windsor. He has written extensively in the area of pastoral and practical theology. His recent publications include *Valuing Age: Pastoral Ministry with Older People* (SPCK, 2008). He is particularly interested in how Christian discipleship nurtures and deepens human well-being. For further information about his work, see his website <www.jameswoodward.info>.

Paula Gooder is a freelance writer and lecturer in biblical studies. She is also a Reader in the Diocese of Birmingham and Canon Theologian of Birmingham and Guildford Cathedrals, as well as a lay Canon of Salisbury Cathedral. Her recent publications include *Searching for Meaning: An Introduction to Interpreting the New Testament* (SPCK, 2008) and *Heaven* (SPCK, 2011).

Mark Pryce is Bishop's Adviser for Clergy Continuing Ministerial Education in the Diocese of Birmingham, and an honorary Canon of Birmingham Cathedral. His other publications include the *Literary Companion to the Lectionary* (2001) and the *Literary Companion for Festivals: Readings for Commemorations Throughout the Year* (2003), both published by SPCK.

CPSIA information can be obtained
at www.ICGtesting.com
Printed in the USA
FFOW01n0819120517
35477FF

9 780664 260217